READING COMPREHENSION SUCCESS
IN 20 MINUTES A DAY

READING COMPREHENSION SUCCESS
IN 20 MINUTES A DAY

3rd Edition

LEARNINGEXPRESS®

NEW YORK

Library of Congress Cataloging-in-Publication Data:
    Reading comprehension success in 20 minutes a day.—3rd ed.
      p. cm.
    ISBN 1-57685-494-9 (paper)
    1. Reading comprehension—Problems, exercises, etc. I. Title. II. Title: Reading
comprehension success in twenty minutes a day.
    LB1050.45.C45 2005
    428.4—dc22

                                    2005047184

Printed in the United States of America

9 8 7 6 5 4 3 2

Third Edition

For information on LearningExpress, other LearningExpress products, or bulk sales, please write to us at:
    LearningExpress
    55 Broadway
    8th Floor
    New York, NY 10006

Or visit us at:
    www.learnatest.com

Contents ▶

CONTENTS

CONTENTS

How to Use This Book ▶

This book is designed to help you improve your reading comprehension skills by studying 20 minutes a day for 20 days. You'll start with the basics and move on to more complex reading comprehension and critical thinking strategies. Please note that although each chapter can be an effective skill builder on its own, it is important that you proceed through this book in order, from Lesson 1 through Lesson 20. Each lesson builds on skills and ideas discussed in the previous chapters. As you move through this book and your reading skills develop, the passages you read will increase both in length and in complexity.

The book begins with a pretest, which will allow you to see how well you can answer various kinds of reading comprehension questions *now,* as you begin. When you finish the book, take the posttest to see how much you've improved.

The text is divided into four sections, each focusing on a different group of related reading and thinking strategies. These strategies will be outlined at the beginning of each section and then reviewed in a special "putting it all together" final lesson.

Each lesson provides several exercises that allow you to practice the skills you learn. To ensure you're on the right track, each lesson also provides answers and explanations for all of the practice questions. Additionally, you will find practical suggestions in each chapter for how to continue practicing these skills in your daily life.

The most important thing you can do to improve your reading skills is to become an active reader. The following guidelines and suggestions outlined will familiarize you with active reading techniques. Use these techniques as much as possible as you work your way through the lessons in this book.

▶ Becoming an Active Reader

Critical reading and thinking skills require active reading. Being an active reader means you have to engage with the text, both mentally and physically.

- Skim ahead and jump back.
- Mark up the text.
- Make specific observations about the text.

Skimming Ahead and Jumping Back

Skimming ahead enables you to see what's coming up in your reading. Page through the text you're about to read. Notice how the text is broken down, what the main topics are, and the order in which they are covered. Notice key words and ideas that are boldfaced, bulleted, boxed, or otherwise highlighted. Skimming through the text beforehand will prepare you for what you are about to read. It's a lot like checking out the hills and curves in the course before a cross-country race. If you know what's ahead, you know how to pace yourself, so you're prepared to handle what's to come.

When you finish your reading, jump back. Review the summaries, headings, and highlighted information in the text. Notice both what the author highlighted and what you highlighted. By jumping back, you help solidify in your mind the ideas and information you just read. You're reminded of how each idea fits into the whole, how ideas and information are connected. When you make connections between ideas, you're much more likely to remember them.

Marking Up the Text

Marking up the text creates a direct physical link between you and the words you're reading. It forces you to pay closer attention to the words you read and takes you to a higher level of comprehension. Use these three strategies to mark up text:

1. Highlight or underline key words and ideas.
2. Circle and define any unfamiliar words or phrases.
3. Record your reactions and questions in the margins.

Highlighting or Underlining Key Ideas

When you highlight or underline key words and ideas, you are identifying the most important parts of the text. There's an important skill at work here: You can't highlight or underline everything, so you have to distinguish between the facts and ideas that are most important (major ideas) and those facts and ideas that are helpful but not so important (minor or supporting ideas). Highlight only the major ideas, so you don't end up with a text that's completely highlighted.

An effectively highlighted text will make for an easy and fruitful review. When you jump back, you'll be quickly reminded of the ideas that are most important to remember. Highlighting or underlining major points as you read also allows you to retain more information from the text.

Circling Unfamiliar Words

One of the most important habits to develop is that of circling and looking up unfamiliar words and phrases. If possible, don't sit down to read without a dictionary by your side. It is not uncommon for the meaning of an entire sentence to hinge on the meaning of a single word or phrase, and if you don't know what that word or phrase means, you won't understand the sentence. Besides, this habit enables you to quickly and steadily expand your vocabulary, so you'll be a more confident reader and speaker.

If you don't have a dictionary readily available, try to determine the meaning of the word as best you can from its context—that is, the words and ideas around it. (There's more on this topic in Lesson 3.) Then, make sure you look up the word as soon as possible so you're sure of its meaning.

Making Marginal Notes

Recording your questions and reactions in the margins turns you from a passive receiver of information into an active participant in a dialogue. (If you're reading a library book, write your reactions in a notebook.) You will get much more out of the ideas and information you read about if you create a "conversation" with the writer. Here are some examples of the kinds of reactions you might write down in the margin or in your notebook:

- **Questions** often come up when you read. They may be answered later in the text, but by that time, you may have forgotten the question! And if your question isn't answered, you may want to discuss it with someone: "Why does the writer describe the new welfare policy as 'unfair'?" or "Why does the character react in this way?"
- **Agreements and disagreements** with the author are bound to arise if you're actively reading. Write them down: "That's not necessarily true!" or "This policy makes a lot of sense to me."
- **Connections** you note can be either between the text and something that you read earlier or between the text and your own experience.
  For example, "I remember feeling the same way when I . . ." or "This is similar to what happened in China."
- **Evaluations** are your way of keeping the author honest. If you think the author isn't providing sufficient support for what he or she is saying or that there's something wrong with that support, say so: "He says the dropping of the bomb was inevitable, but he doesn't explain why" or "This is a very selfish reason."

Making Observations

Good readers know that writers use many different strategies to express their ideas. Even if you know very little about those strategies, you can make useful observations about what you read to better understand and remember the author's ideas. You can notice, for example, the author's choice of words; the structure of the sentences and paragraphs; any repetition of words or ideas; important details about people, places, and things; and so on.

This step—making observations—is essential because your observations (what you notice) lead you to logical inferences about what you read. *Inferences* are conclusions based on reason, fact, or evidence. You are constantly making inferences based on your observations, even when you're not reading. For example, if you notice that the sky is full of dark, heavy clouds, you might infer that it is going to rain; if you notice that your coworker has a stack of gardening books on her desk, you might infer that she likes gardening.

If you misunderstand what you read, it is often because you haven't looked closely enough at the text. As a result, you base your inferences on your own ideas and experiences, not on what's actually written in the text. You end up forcing your own ideas on the author (rather than listening to what the author has to say) and then forming your own ideas about it. It's critical, then, that you begin to really pay attention to what writers say and how they say it.

If any of this sounds confusing now, don't worry. Each of these ideas will be thoroughly explained in the lessons that follow. In the meantime, start practicing active reading as best you can. Begin by taking the pretest.

READING
COMPREHENSION
SUCCESS
IN 20 MINUTES A DAY

Pretest ▶

Before you start your study of reading skills, you may want to get an idea of how much you already know and how much you need to learn. If that's the case, take the pretest that follows. The pretest consists of 50 multiple-choice questions covering all the lessons in this book. Naturally, 50 questions can't cover every single concept or strategy you will learn by working through this book. So even if you get all the questions on the pretest right, it's almost guaranteed that you will find a few ideas or reading tactics in this book that you didn't already know. On the other hand, if you get many questions wrong on this pretest, don't despair. This book will show you how to read more effectively, step by step.

You should use this pretest to get a general idea of how much you already know. If you get a high score, you may be able to spend less time with this book than you originally planned. If you get a low score, you may find that you will need more than 20 minutes a day to get through each chapter and improve your reading skills.

There's an answer sheet you can use for filling in the correct answers on page 3. Or, if you prefer, simply circle the answer numbers in this book. If the book doesn't belong to you, write the numbers 1–50 on a piece of paper and record your answers there. Take as much time as you need to do this short test. When you finish, check your answers against the answer key at the end of this lesson. Each answer offers the lesson(s) in this book that teaches you about the reading strategy in that question.

1.	ⓐ	ⓑ	ⓒ	ⓓ
2.	ⓐ	ⓑ	ⓒ	ⓓ
3.	ⓐ	ⓑ	ⓒ	ⓓ
4.	ⓐ	ⓑ	ⓒ	ⓓ
5.	ⓐ	ⓑ	ⓒ	ⓓ
6.	ⓐ	ⓑ	ⓒ	ⓓ
7.	ⓐ	ⓑ	ⓒ	ⓓ
8.	ⓐ	ⓑ	ⓒ	ⓓ
9.	ⓐ	ⓑ	ⓒ	ⓓ
10.	ⓐ	ⓑ	ⓒ	ⓓ
11.	ⓐ	ⓑ	ⓒ	ⓓ
12.	ⓐ	ⓑ	ⓒ	ⓓ
13.	ⓐ	ⓑ	ⓒ	ⓓ
14.	ⓐ	ⓑ	ⓒ	ⓓ
15.	ⓐ	ⓑ	ⓒ	ⓓ
16.	ⓐ	ⓑ	ⓒ	ⓓ
17.	ⓐ	ⓑ	ⓒ	ⓓ

18.	ⓐ	ⓑ	ⓒ	ⓓ
19.	ⓐ	ⓑ	ⓒ	ⓓ
20.	ⓐ	ⓑ	ⓒ	ⓓ
21.	ⓐ	ⓑ	ⓒ	ⓓ
22.	ⓐ	ⓑ	ⓒ	ⓓ
23.	ⓐ	ⓑ	ⓒ	ⓓ
24.	ⓐ	ⓑ	ⓒ	ⓓ
25.	ⓐ	ⓑ	ⓒ	ⓓ
26.	ⓐ	ⓑ	ⓒ	ⓓ
27.	ⓐ	ⓑ	ⓒ	ⓓ
28.	ⓐ	ⓑ	ⓒ	ⓓ
29.	ⓐ	ⓑ	ⓒ	ⓓ
30.	ⓐ	ⓑ	ⓒ	ⓓ
31.	ⓐ	ⓑ	ⓒ	ⓓ
32.	ⓐ	ⓑ	ⓒ	ⓓ
33.	ⓐ	ⓑ	ⓒ	ⓓ
34.	ⓐ	ⓑ	ⓒ	ⓓ

35.	ⓐ	ⓑ	ⓒ	ⓓ
36.	ⓐ	ⓑ	ⓒ	ⓓ
37.	ⓐ	ⓑ	ⓒ	ⓓ
38.	ⓐ	ⓑ	ⓒ	ⓓ
39.	ⓐ	ⓑ	ⓒ	ⓓ
40.	ⓐ	ⓑ	ⓒ	ⓓ
41.	ⓐ	ⓑ	ⓒ	ⓓ
42.	ⓐ	ⓑ	ⓒ	ⓓ
43.	ⓐ	ⓑ	ⓒ	ⓓ
44.	ⓐ	ⓑ	ⓒ	ⓓ
45.	ⓐ	ⓑ	ⓒ	ⓓ
46.	ⓐ	ⓑ	ⓒ	ⓓ
47.	ⓐ	ⓑ	ⓒ	ⓓ
48.	ⓐ	ⓑ	ⓒ	ⓓ
49.	ⓐ	ⓑ	ⓒ	ⓓ
50.	ⓐ	ⓑ	ⓒ	ⓓ

► Pretest

The pretest consists of a series of reading passages with questions that follow to test your comprehension.

Cultural Center Adds Classes for Young Adults

The Allendale Cultural Center has expanded its arts program to include classes for young adults. Director Leah Martin announced Monday that beginning in September, three new classes will be offered to the Allendale community. The course titles will be Yoga for Teenagers; Hip Hop Dance: Learning the Latest Moves; and Creative Journaling for Teens: Discovering the Writer Within. The latter course will not be held at the Allendale Cultural Center but instead will meet at the Allendale Public Library.

Staff member Tricia Cousins will teach the yoga and hip hop classes. Ms. Cousins is an accomplished choreographer as well as an experienced dance educator. She has an MA in dance education from Teachers College, Columbia University, where she wrote a thesis on the pedagogical effectiveness of dance education. The journaling class will be taught by Betsy Milford. Ms. Milford is the head librarian at the Allendale Public Library as well as a columnist for the professional journal *Library Focus.*

The courses are part of the Allendale Cultural Center's Project Teen, which was initiated by Leah Martin, Director of the Cultural Center. According to Martin, this project is a direct result of her efforts to make the center a more integral part of the Allendale community. Over the last several years, the number of people who have visited the cultural center for classes or events has steadily declined. Project Teen is primarily funded by a munificent grant from The McGee Arts Foundation, an organization devoted to bringing arts programs to young adults. Martin oversees the Project Teen board, which consists of five board members. Two board members are students at Allendale's Brookdale High School; the other three are adults with backgrounds in education and the arts.

The creative journaling class will be cosponsored by Brookdale High School, and students who complete the class will be given the opportunity to publish one of their journal entries in *Pulse,* Brookdale's student literary magazine. Students who complete the hip hop class will be eligible to participate in the Allendale Review, an annual concert sponsored by the cultural center that features local actors, musicians, and dancers.

All classes are scheduled to begin immediately following school dismissal, and transportation will be available from Brookdale High School to the Allendale Cultural Center and the Allendale Public Library. For more information about Project Teen, contact the cultural center's programming office at 988-0099 or drop by the office after June 1 to pick up a fall course catalog. The office is located on the third floor of the Allendale Town Hall.

1. The Creative Journaling for Teens class will be cosponsored by
  a. The Allendale Public Library.
  b. The McGee Arts Foundation.
  c. Brookdale High School.
  d. Betsy Milford.

2. Which of the following statements is correct?
  a. Tricia Cousins will teach two of the new classes.
  b. The new classes will begin on June 1.
  c. People who want a complete fall catalogue should stop by the Allendale Public Library.
  d. The cultural center's annual concert is called *Pulse.*

3. According to Leah Martin, what was the direct cause of Project Teen?
   a. Tricia Cousins, the talented choreographer and dance educator, was available to teach courses in the fall.
   b. Community organizations were ignoring local teenagers.
   c. The McGee Arts Foundation wanted to be more involved in Allendale's arts programming.
   d. She wanted to make the cultural center a more important part of the Allendale community.

4. Which of the following factors is implied as another reason for Project Teen?
   a. The number of people who have visited the cultural center has declined over the last several years.
   b. The cultural center wanted a grant from The McGee Arts Foundation.
   c. The young people of Allendale have complained about the cultural center's offerings.
   d. Leah Martin thinks classes for teenagers are more important than classes for adults.

5. From the context of the passage, it can be determined that the word "munificent" most nearly means
   a. complicated.
   b. generous.
   c. curious.
   d. unusual.

6. The title of the course "Creative Journaling for Teens: Discovering the Writer Within" implies that
   a. all young people should write in a journal daily.
   b. teenagers do not have enough hobbies.
   c. writing in a journal can help teenagers become better and more creative writers.
   d. teenagers are in need of guidance and direction.

7. Which of the following correctly states the primary subject of this article?
   a. Leah Martin's personal ideas about young adults
   b. The McGee Foundation's grant to the Allendale Cultural Center
   c. three new classes for young adults added to the cultural center's arts program
   d. the needs of young adults in Allendale

8. This article is organized in which of the following ways?
   a. in chronological order, from the past to the future
   b. most important information first, followed by background and details.
   c. background first, followed by the most important information and details.
   d. as sensational news, with the most controversial topic first

(excerpt from the opening of an untitled essay)

John Steinbeck's *Grapes of Wrath*, published in 1939, was followed ten years later by A.B. Guthrie's *The Way West*. Both books chronicle a migration, though that of Guthrie's pioneers is considerably less bleak in origin. What strikes one at first glance, however, are the commonalities. Both Steinbeck's and Guthrie's characters are primarily farmers. They look to their destinations with nearly religious enthusiasm, imagining their "promised" land the way the Biblical Israelites envisioned Canaan. Both undergo great hardship to make the trek. But the two sagas differ distinctly in origin. Steinbeck's Oklahomans are forced off their land by the banks who own their mortgages, and they follow a false promise—that jobs await them as seasonal laborers in California. Guthrie's farmers willingly remove themselves, selling their land and trading their old dreams for their new hope in Oregon. The pioneers' decision to leave their farms in Missouri and the East is frivolous and ill-founded in comparison with the Oklahomans' unwilling response to displacement. Yet, it is they, the pioneers, whom our history books declare the heroes.

9. From the context of the passage, it can be determined that the word "frivolous" most nearly means
a. silly.
b. high-minded.
c. difficult.
d. calculated.

10. Suppose that the author is considering following this sentence with supportive detail: "Both undergo great hardship to make the trek." Which of the following sentences would be in keeping with the comparison and contrast structure of the paragraph?
a. The migrants in *The Way West* cross the Missouri, then the Kaw, and make their way overland to the Platte.
b. The Oklahomans' jalopies break down repeatedly, while the pioneers' wagons need frequent repairs.
c. Today's travelers would consider it a hardship to spend several days, let alone several months, getting anywhere.
d. The Joad family, in *The Grapes of Wrath*, loses both grandmother and grandfather before the journey is complete.

11. Which of the following excerpts from the essay is an opinion, rather than a fact?
a. "Both Steinbeck's and Guthrie's characters are primarily farmers."
b. "Steinbeck's Oklahomans are forced off their land by the banks who own their mortgages…"
c. "John Steinbeck's *Grapes of Wrath*, published in 1939, was followed ten years later by A.B. Guthrie's *The Way West*."
d. "The pioneers' decision to leave their farms in Missouri and the East is frivolous and ill-founded in comparison with the Oklahomans'…"

12. The language in the paragraph implies that which of the following will happen to the Oklahomans when they arrive in California?
a. They will find a means to practice their religion freely.
b. They will be declared national heroes.
c. They will not find the jobs they were promised.
d. They will make their livings as mechanics rather than as farm laborers.

Bill Clinton's Inaugural Address
(excerpt from the opening)

When George Washington first took the oath I have just sworn to uphold, news traveled slowly across the land by horseback and across the ocean by boat. Now the sights and sounds of this ceremony are broadcast instantaneously to billions around the world. Communications and commerce are global. Investment is mobile. Technology is almost magical, and ambition for a better life is now universal.

We earn our livelihood in America today in peaceful competition with people all across the Earth. Profound and powerful forces are shaking and remaking our world, and the urgent question of our time is whether we can make change our friend and not our enemy. This new world has already enriched the lives of millions of Americans who are able to compete and win in it. But when most people are working harder for less; when others cannot work at all; when the cost of healthcare devastates families and threatens to bankrupt our enterprises, great and small; when the fear of crime robs law-abiding citizens of their freedom; and when millions of poor children cannot even imagine the lives we are calling them to lead, we have not made change our friend.

13. What is the central topic of the speech so far?
   a. how Americans can keep up with global competition
   b. ways in which technology has undermined our economy
   c. ways in which technology has improved our lives
   d. how change has affected America and our need to adapt

14. By comparing our times with those of George Washington, Bill Clinton demonstrates
   a. how apparently different, but actually similar, the two eras are.
   b. how technology has drastically speeded up communications.
   c. that presidential inaugurations receive huge media attention.
   d. that television is a much more convincing communications tool than print.

15. When President Clinton says that "most people are working harder for less," he is
   a. reaching a reasonable conclusion based on evidence he has provided.
   b. reaching an unreasonable conclusion based on evidence he has provided.
   c. making a generalization that would require evidence before it could be confirmed.
   d. making a generalization that is so obvious that evidence is not needed.

16. Assuming that Clinton wants to add something about crime being a more serious threat in our time than in George Washington's, which of the following sentences would be most consistent with the tone of the presidential speech?
   a. If I'd been alive in George's day, I would have enjoyed knowing that my wife and child could walk city streets without being mugged.
   b. In George Washington's time, Americans may not have enjoyed as many luxuries, but they could rest in the awareness that their neighborhoods were safe.
   c. George could at least count on one thing. He knew that his family was safe from crime.
   d. A statistical analysis of the overall growth in crime rates since 1789 would reveal that a significant increase has occurred.

The Crossing
Chapter I: The Blue Wall
(excerpt from the opening of a novel by Winston Churchill)

I was born under the Blue Ridge, and under that side which is blue in the evening light, in a wild land of game and forest and rushing waters. There, on the borders of a creek that runs into the Yadkin River, in a cabin that was chinked with red mud, I came into the world a subject of King George the Third, in that part of his realm known as the province of North Carolina.

The cabin reeked of corn-pone and bacon, and the odor of pelts. It had two shakedowns, on one of which I slept under a bearskin. A rough stone chimney was reared outside, and the fireplace was as long as my father was tall. There was a crane in it, and a bake kettle; and over it great buckhorns held my father's rifle when it was not in use. On other horns hung jerked bear's meat and venison hams, and gourds for drinking cups, and bags of seed, and my father's best hunting shirt; also, in a neglected corner, several articles of woman's attire from pegs. These once belonged to my mother. Among them was a gown of silk, of a fine, faded pattern, over which I was wont to speculate. The women at the Cross-Roads, twelve miles away, were dressed in coarse butternut wool and huge sunbonnets. But when I questioned my father on these matters he would give me no answers.

My father was—how shall I say what he was? To this day I can only surmise many things of him. He was a Scotchman born, and I know now that he had a slight Scotch accent. At the time of which I write, my early childhood, he was a frontiersman and hunter. I can see him now, with his hunting shirt and leggins and moccasins; his powder horn, engraved with wondrous scenes; his bullet pouch and tomahawk and hunting knife. He was a tall, lean man with a strange, sad face. And he talked little save when he drank too many "horns," as they were called in that country. These lapses of my father's were a perpetual source of wonder to me—and, I must say, of delight. They occurred only when a passing traveler who hit his fancy chanced that way, or, what was almost as rare, a neighbor. Many a winter night I have lain awake under the skins, listening to a flow of language that held me spellbound, though I understood scarce a word of it.

"Virtuous and vicious every man must be,
Few in the extreme, but all in a degree."

The chance neighbor or traveler was no less struck with wonder. And many the time have I heard the query, at the Cross-Roads and elsewhere, "Whar Alec Trimble got his larnin'?"

17. Why did the narrator enjoy it when his father drank too many "horns," or drafts of liquor?
 a. The father spoke brilliantly at those times.
 b. The boy was then allowed to do as he pleased.
 c. These were the only times when the father was not abusive.
 d. The boy was allowed to sample the drink himself.

18. Judging by the sentences surrounding it, the word "surmise" in the third paragraph most nearly means
 a. to form a negative opinion.
 b. to praise.
 c. to desire.
 d. to guess.

19. The mention of the dress in the second paragraph is most likely meant to
   a. show the similarity between its owner and other members of the community.
   b. show how warm the climate was.
   c. show the dissimilarity between its owner and other members of the community.
   d. give us insight into the way most of the women of the region dressed.

20. It can be inferred from the passage that Alec Trimble is
   a. a traveler.
   b. a neighbor.
   c. the narrator's father.
   d. a poet.

21. What is the meaning of the lines of verse quoted in the passage?
   a. Men who pretend to be virtuous are actually vicious.
   b. Moderate amounts of virtuousness and viciousness are present in all men.
   c. Virtuous men cannot also be vicious.
   d. Whether men are virtuous or vicious depends on the difficulty of their circumstances.

22. Which of the following adjectives best describes the region in which the cabin is located?
   a. remote
   b. urban
   c. agricultural
   d. flat

23. The author most likely uses dialect when quoting the question, "Whar Alec Trimble got his larnin'?" in order to
   a. show disapproval of the father's drinking.
   b. show how people talked down to the narrator.
   c. show the speakers' lack of education.
   d. mimic the way the father talked.

(excerpt from a letter to a pet-sitter)

Dear Lee,

As I told you, I'll be gone until Wednesday morning. Thank you so much for taking on my "children" while I'm away. Like real children, they can be kind of irritating sometimes, but I'm going to enjoy myself so much more knowing they're getting some kind human attention. Remember that Regina (the "queen" in Latin, and she acts like one) is teething. If you don't watch her, she'll chew anything, including her sister, the cat. There are plenty of chew toys around the house. Whenever she starts gnawing on anything illegal, just divert her with one of those. She generally settles right down to a good hour-long chew. Then you'll see her wandering around whimpering with the remains of the toy in her mouth. She gets really frustrated because what she wants is to bury the thing. She'll try to dig a hole between the cushions of the couch. Finding that unsatisfactory, she'll wander some more, discontent, until you solve her problem for her. I usually show her the laundry basket, moving a few clothes so she can bury her toy beneath them. I do sound like a parent, don't I? You have to understand, my own son is practically grown up.

Regina's food is the Puppy Chow in the utility room, where the other pet food is stored. Give her a bowl once in the morning and once in the evening. No more than that, no matter how much she begs. Beagles are notorious overeaters, according to her breeder, and I don't want her to lose her girlish figure. She can share Rex (the King's) water, but be sure it's changed daily. She needs to go out several times a day, especially last thing at night and first thing in the morning. Let her stay out for about ten minutes each time, so she can do *all* her business. She also needs a walk in the afternoon, after which it's important to romp with her for awhile in the yard. The game she loves most is fetch, but be sure to make her drop the ball. She'd rather play tug of war with it. Tell her, "Sit!" Then, when she does, say, "Drop it!" Be sure to tell her "good girl," and then throw the ball for her. I hope you'll enjoy these sessions as much as I do.

Now, for the other two, Rex and Paws… (*letter continues*)

24. The tone of this letter is best described as
  a. chatty and humorous.
  b. logical and precise.
  c. confident and trusting.
  d. condescending and preachy.

25. If the pet-sitter is a business-like professional who watches people's pets for a living, she or he would likely prefer
  a. more first-person revelations about the owner.
  b. fewer first-person revelations about the owner.
  c. more praise for agreeing to watch the animals.
  d. greater detail on the animals' cute behavior.

26. According to the author, his or her attachment to the pets derives at least partially from
  a. their regal pedigrees and royal bearing.
  b. having few friends to pass the time with.
  c. these particular animals' exceptional needs.
  d. a desire to continue parenting.

27. The information in the note is sufficient to determine that there are three animals. They are
  a. two cats and a dog.
  b. three dogs.
  c. a dog, a cat, and an unspecified animal.
  d. a cat, a dog, and a parrot.

28. Given that there are three animals to feed, which of the following arrangements of the feeding instructions would be most efficient and easiest to follow?
   a. all given in one list, chronologically from morning to night
   b. provided separately as they are for Regina, within separate passages on each animal
   c. given in the order of quantities needed, the most to the least
   d. placed in the middle of the letter, where they would be least likely to be overlooked

29. From the context of the note, it is most likely that the name "Rex" is
   a. Spanish.
   b. English.
   c. French.
   d. Latin.

30. If the sitter is to follow the owner's directions in playing fetch with Regina, at what point will he or she will tell Regina "good girl"?
   a. every time Regina goes after the ball
   b. after Regina finds the ball
   c. when Regina brings the ball back
   d. after Regina drops the ball

(excerpt from a pro-voting essay)

Voting is the privilege for which wars have been fought, protests have been organized, and editorials have been written. "No taxation without representation" was a battle cry of the American Revolution. Women struggled for suffrage as did all minorities. Eighteen-year-olds clamored for the right to vote, saying that if they were old enough to go to war, they should be allowed to vote. Yet Americans have a deplorable voting history.

Interviewing people about their voting habits is revealing. There are individuals who state that they have never voted. Often, they claim that their individual vote doesn't matter. Some people blame their absence from the voting booth on the fact that they do not know enough about the issues. In a democracy, we can express our opinions to our elected leaders, but more than half of us sometimes avoid choosing the people who make the policies that affect our lives.

31. This argument relies primarily on which of the following techniques to make its points?
   a. emotional assertions
   b. researched facts in support of an assertion
   c. emotional appeals to voters
   d. emotional appeals to nonvoters

32. Which of the following sentences best summarizes the main idea of the passage?
   a. Americans are too lazy to vote.
   b. Women and minorities fought for their right to vote.
   c. Americans do not take voting seriously enough.
   d. Americans do not think that elected officials take their opinions seriously.

33. By choosing the word "clamored," the author implies that
   a. eighteen-year-olds are generally enthusiastic.
   b. voting was not a serious concern to eighteen-year-olds.
   c. eighteen-year-olds felt strongly that they should be allowed to vote.
   d. eighteen-year-olds do not handle themselves in an adult-like manner.

Improving Streamside Wildlife Habitats
(excerpt from Habitat Extension Bulletin distributed by the
Wyoming Game and Fish Department)

Riparian vegetation [the green band of vegetation along a watercourse] can help stabilize stream banks; filter sediment from surface runoff; and provide wildlife habitat, livestock forage, and scenic value. Well-developed vegetation also allows bank soils to absorb extra water during spring runoff, releasing it later during drier months, thus improving late-summer stream flows.

In many parts of the arid West, trees and shrubs are found only in riparian areas. Woody plants are very important as winter cover for many wildlife species, including upland game birds such as pheasants and turkeys. Often this winter cover is the greatest single factor limiting game bird populations. Woody vegetation also provides hiding cover and browse for many other species of birds and mammals, both game and nongame.

Dead trees ("snags") are an integral part of streamside habitats and should be left standing whenever possible. Woodpeckers, nuthatches, brown creepers, and other birds eat the insects that decompose the wood. These insects usually pose no threat to nearby living trees. Occasionally a disease organism or misuse of pesticides will weaken or kill a stand of trees. If several trees in a small area begin to die, contact your local extension agent immediately.

34. What is the effect of the word choice "riparian"?
   a. It gives the article an authoritative, scientific tone.
   b. It causes confusion, since both streams and rivers could be viewed as riparian.
   c. It seems condescending, as if the author was stooping to teach readers.
   d. It misleads readers into thinking they are getting scientific information when they are not.

35. By listing the specific birds that live in riparian areas, the author conveys a sense of
   a. urgency on behalf of endangered species.
   b. the rich and varied life in such areas.
   c. his or her own importance as a scientific expert.
   d. poetic wonder over the variety found in nature.

36. Assume that the author has done some other writing on this topic for a different audience. The other piece begins: "Remember the last time you walked along a stream? No doubt thick vegetation prevented easy progress." What is the likely effect on the reader of this opening?
   a. an aroused interest, due to the reference to the reader's personal experience
   b. resentment, due to being addressed so personally
   c. loss of interest, because the opening line makes no attempt to draw the reader in
   d. confusion, because not every reader has walked along a stream

37. The main subject of the second paragraph of this passage is
   a. the types of birds that live in riparian areas.
   b. the effect of winter cover on water purity.
   c. the role of trees and shrubs in riparian areas.
   d. how winter cover affects game bird populations.

38. Overall, the assertions of this passage seem to be based on
- **a.** rash opinion with little observation behind it.
- **b.** deeply held emotional convictions.
- **c.** fact derived from scientific literature.
- **d.** inconclusive evidence gathered in field studies.

39. What does the word "arid" accomplish in the first sentence of the second paragraph?
- **a.** It provides a sense of the generally high altitude of the West.
- **b.** It signifies a change in subject from the Eastern United States to the West.
- **c.** It clarifies the author's purpose to discuss nonurban areas.
- **d.** It clarifies the reason that trees and shrubs are found only in riparian areas.

(excerpt from "First," a short story)

First, you ought to know that I'm "only" fourteen. My mother points this out frequently. I can make decisions for myself when I'm old enough to vote, she says. Second, I should tell you that she's right—I'm not always responsible. I sometimes take the prize for a grade-A dork. Last weekend, for instance, when I was staying at Dad's, I decided it was time I learned to drive. It was Sunday morning, 7 A.M. to be exact, and I hadn't slept well thinking about this argument I'll be telling you about in a minute. Nobody was up yet in the neighborhood, and I thought there would be no harm in backing the car out of the garage and cruising around the block. But Dad has a clutch car, and the "R" on the shift handle was up on the left side, awful close to first gear, and I guess you can guess the rest.

Dad's always been understanding. He didn't say, like Mom would, "Okay, little Miss Know-It-All, you can just spend the rest of the year paying this off." He worried about what might have happened to *me*—to *me*, you see, and that made me feel more guilty than anything. Overall, I just think he'd be a better number-one caregiver, if you get my drift. Of course I can't say things like that to Mom.

To her, I have to say, "But Mom, Dad's place is closer to school. I could ride my bike."

She replies, "Jennifer Lynn, you don't own a bike, because you left it in the yard and it was stolen, and you haven't got the perseverance it takes to do a little work and earn the money to replace it."

40. Which description best explains the structure of the story so far?
- **a.** chronological, according to what happens first, second, and so on
- **b.** reverse chronological order, with the most recent events recorded first
- **c.** intentionally confused order, incorporating flashbacks to previous events
- **d.** according to importance, with the most significant details related first

41. What device does the author use to illustrate the narrator's feelings about her mother and father?
- **a.** vivid and specific visual detail
- **b.** rhetorical questions, which make a point but don't invite a direct answer
- **c.** metaphors and other figurative language
- **d.** contrast between the parents' typical reactions

42. The narrator attributes her inability to sleep when staying at her father's house to
   a. thinking about a disagreement with someone.
   b. the uncomfortable quiet of an early Sunday morning.
   c. the sore throat she had from shouting so much.
   d. her accident with the car.

43. The first-person point of view in this story
   a. obscures how the narrator's mind works.
   b. illustrates the thoughts and personality of the narrator.
   c. makes the narrator seem distant and rigid.
   d. gives us direct access to the minds of all the characters.

44. When the narrator says she sometimes "take[s] the prize for a grade-A dork," the word choice is intended to indicate
   a. that she doesn't know proper English.
   b. her age and culture.
   c. that she is unable to judge her own actions.
   d. that she thinks she's better than most others who might be termed "dorks".

45. From the context in the last sentence of the passage, it can be determined that the word "perseverance" most nearly means
   a. attractiveness.
   b. thinking ability.
   c. ability to persist.
   d. love of danger.

46. Overall, this narrator's tone is best described as
   a. emotional and familiar.
   b. stuck up and superior.
   c. argumentative and tactless.
   d. pleasant and reassuring.

47. In choosing to use the bike argument with her mother, the narrator is trying to appeal to her mother's
   a. compassion over her lost bike.
   b. disregard for material objects.
   c. laziness.
   d. reason.

48. The main argument the narrator has been having with her mother is over whether she should
   a. be allowed to date.
   b. live with her mother or father.
   c. be allowed to drive a car.
   d. pay for things she breaks.

49. It appears that the mother has alienated her daughter by
   a. being too busy to give her the attention she needs.
   b. having divorced her father.
   c. insisting too much on reasonableness.
   d. valuing things over people and feelings.

50. What most likely happened with the car?
   a. The narrator mistook first gear for reverse and ran into the garage wall.
   b. The narrator stole it from her father and drove it over to her mother's.
   c. The father left it in gear, and when the narrator started it, it leapt forward into the wall.
   d. The narrator attempted suicide through carbon monoxide poisoning.

▶ Answer Key

If you miss any of the answers, you can find help for that kind of question in the lesson(s) shown to the right of the answer.

1. c. Lesson 1	**26.** d. Lesson 9
2. a. Lesson 1	**27.** c. Lesson 1
3. d. Lesson 9	**28.** a. Lessons 6 and 10
4. a. Lesson 16	**29.** d. Lesson 3
5. b. Lesson 3	**30.** d. Lesson 6
6. c. Lesson 12	**31.** b. Lesson 18
7. c. Lesson 2	**32.** c. Lesson 2
8. b. Lessons 6 and 7	**33.** c. Lesson 12
9. a. Lesson 3	**34.** a. Lesson 12
10. b. Lesson 8	**35.** b. Lesson 13
11. d. Lesson 4	**36.** a. Lesson 11
12. c. Lesson 17	**37.** c. Lesson 2
13. d. Lesson 2	**38.** c. Lesson 4
14. b. Lesson 8	**39.** d. Lesson 3
15. c. Lesson 4	**40.** c. Lessons 6, 7, and 10
16. b. Lesson 13	**41.** d. Lesson 8
17. a. Lesson 19	**42.** a. Lesson 9
18. d. Lesson 3	**43.** b. Lesson 11
19. c. Lesson 8	**44.** b. Lesson 12
20. c. Lesson 19	**45.** c. Lesson 3
21. b. Lesson 19	**46.** a. Lesson 14
22. a. Lesson 16	**47.** d. Lesson 18
23. c. Lesson 13	**48.** b. Lesson 16
24. a. Lesson 14	**49.** d. Lesson 17
25. b. Lesson 11	**50.** a. Lesson 17

Building a Strong Foundation

You may not have thought of it this way before, but critical readers are a lot like crime scene investigators. In their search for the truth, they do not let opinions sway them; they want to know what actually happened. They collect tangible evidence and facts and use this information to draw an informed conclusion. Separating fact from opinion is essential during a crime scene investigation. It is also a crucial skill for effective reading.

When you read, look for clues to understand the author's meaning. What is this passage about? What is this writer saying? What is his or her message? At times, it may seem like authors are trying to hide their meaning from you. But no matter how complex a piece of writing may be, the author always leaves plenty of clues for the careful reader to find. It is your job to find those clues. Be a good detective when you read. Open your eyes and ask the right questions. In other words, read carefully and actively.

The five lessons that follow cover the basics of reading comprehension. By the end of this section, you should be able to:

- Find the basic facts in a passage
- Determine the main idea of a passage
- Determine the meaning of unfamiliar words from context
- Distinguish between fact and opinion

Getting the Essential Information

LESSON SUMMARY

The first step in increasing your reading comprehension is to learn how to get the basic information. Like a good detective, start with the basic facts. To get the facts, be an active reader and look for clues as you read.

magine, for a moment, that you are a detective. You have just been called to the scene of a crime; a house has been robbed. What's the first thing you should do when you arrive?

    a. See what's on the TV.
    b. Check what's in the fridge.
    c. Get the basic facts of the case.

The answer, of course, is **c**, get the basic facts of the case: the who, what, when, where, how, and why. What happened? To whom? When? Where? How did it happen? And why?

As a reader faced with a text, you go through a similar process. The first thing you should do is establish the facts. What does this piece of writing tell you? What happens? To whom? When, where, how, and why? If you can answer these basic questions, you're on your way to really comprehending what you read. (You'll work on answering the more difficult question—"*Why* did it happen?"—in Lesson 2.)

► What Are the Facts?

Let's start with a definition. A **fact** is:

- Something that we know for certain to have happened
- Something that we know for certain to be true
- Something that we know for certain to exist

Much of what you read, especially today in this "Information Age," is designed to provide you with facts. You may read, for example, about a new office procedure that you must follow; about how the new computer system works; about what happened at the staff meeting. If you're taking a standardized test, you'll probably have to answer reading comprehension ques-tions that ask about the facts in a reading passage. These facts are not always easy to determine, especially if the writing is dense or complicated. To make it simpler, ask yourself these questions as you read: What facts am I expected to know? What am I to learn or be aware of? What happened? What is true? What exists?

Practice Passage 1

Jump right into the task of finding facts. The following brief passage is similar to something you might see in a newspaper. Read the passage carefully, and then answer the questions that follow. Remember, careful reading is active reading (see the Introduction), so mark up the text as you go. Underline key words and ideas; circle and define any unfamiliar words or phrases; and record your reactions and questions in the margins.

On Friday, October 21, at approximately 8:30 A.M., Judith Reynolds, owner of The Cupcake Factory, arrived at her establishment to find that it had been robbed and vandalized overnight. The front window of the shop at 128 Broad Street was broken, and chairs and tables were overturned throughout the café area. Additionally, the cash register had been pried open and emptied of money. The thieves attempted to open the safe as well, but were unsuccessful. Ms. Reynolds used her cell phone to report the crime to the police. She also phoned the proprietor of Primo Pizza, located at 130 Broad Street, as she noticed that the door of that restaurant showed signs of forced entry. The police department is asking anyone with information to call 555-2323.

1. What happened to The Cupcake Factory?

2. When was the crime discovered?

3. Where did it happen?

4. What was stolen?

5. Who called the police?

6. What other businesses were affected?

Remember, good reading is active reading. Did you mark up the passage? If so, it may have looked something like this:

when

who

On Friday, October 21, at approximately 8:30 A.M., Judith Reynolds, owner of
The Cupcake Factory, arrived at her establishment to find that it had been
robbed and vandalized overnight. The front window of the shop at 128 Broad
Street was broken, and chairs and tables were overturned throughout the café
area. Additionally, the cash register had been pried open and emptied of money.
The thieves attempted to open the safe as well, but were unsuccessful. Ms.
Reynolds used her cell phone to report the crime to the police. She also phoned
the proprietor of Primo Pizza, located at 130 Broad Street, as she noticed that the
door of that restaurant showed signs of forced entry. The police department is
asking anyone with information to call 555-2323.

what happened—robbery and vandalization

interesting detail

another business was affected

where

what a mess! money was stolen

unclear if anything was taken from Primo Pizza from this report

You'll notice that the answers to the questions have all been underlined, because these are the key words and ideas in this passage. But here are the answers in a more conventional form.

1. What happened to The Cupcake Factory? *It was robbed and vandalized.*

2. When was the crime discovered? *At 8:30 A.M. on Friday, October 21.*

3. Where did it happen? *128 Broad Street.*

4. What was stolen? *Money from the cash register.*

5. Who called the police? *Judith Reynolds, owner of The Cupcake Factory.*

6. What other businesses were affected? *Possibly Primo Pizza.*

Notice that these questions went beyond the basic who, what, when, and where to include some of the details, like why the proprietor of the restaurant next door was called. This is because details in reading comprehension, as well as in detective work, can be very important clues that may help answer the remaining questions: Who did it, how, and why?

Practice Passage 2

This passage includes instructions for renewing a driver's license. Read it carefully and answer the questions that follow.

Instructions for License Renewal

A driver's license must be renewed every four years. A renewal application is sent approximately five to seven weeks before the expiration date listed on the license. Individuals who fail to renew within three years of the license expiration date are not eligible for a renewal and must repeat the initial licensing process. To renew a license, you must visit a Motor Vehicles Agency. You must present a completed renewal application; your current driver's license; acceptable proof of age, identification, and address; and proof of social security in the form of a social security card, a state or federal income tax return, a current pay stub, or a W-2 form. You must also pay the required fee. If all the documents and payment are in order, your photo will be taken and a new license will be issued.

7. What documents does one need to renew a driver's license?

8. What documents represent proof of social security?

9. How often must one renew a driver's license?

10. How does one obtain the renewal form?

11. True or False: You can renew your driver's license by mail.

Before you look at the answers, look at the next page to see how you might have marked up the passage to highlight the important information.

Instructions for License Renewal

how often I need to renew

A driver's license must be renewed every four years. A renewal application is sent — *application will be mailed*

approximately five to seven weeks before the expiration date listed on the license.

Individuals who fail to renew within three years of the license expiration date are

not eligible for a renewal and must repeat the initial licensing process. To renew

must go in person. find out nearest location — a license, you must visit a Motor Vehicles Agency. You must present a completed

renewal application; your current driver's license; acceptable proof of age, iden-

tification, and address; and proof of social security in the form of a social secu- — *documents needed for renewal*

rity card, a state or federal income tax return, a current pay stub, or a W-2 form.

You must also pay the required fee. If all the documents and payment are in order,

your photo will be taken and a new license will be issued.

bring checkbook!

With a marked-up text like this, it's very easy to find the answers.

7. What documents does one need to renew a driver's license?
> *Completed renewal application*
> *Current driver's license*
> *Acceptable proof of age, identification, and address*
> *Proof of social security*
> *Money to pay required fee*

8. What documents represent proof of social security?
> *Social security card*
> *State or federal income tax return*
> *Current pay stub*
> *W-2 form*

9. How often must one renew a driver's license? *Every four years.*

10. How does one obtain the renewal form? *It is sent five to seven weeks before current license expires.*

11. True or False: You can renew your driver's license by mail. *False: You can only renew by visiting a Motor Vehicles Agency.*

Practice Passage 3

Now look at one more short passage. Again, read carefully and answer the questions that follow.

Today's postal service is more efficient and reliable than ever before. Mail that used to take months to move by horse and foot now moves around the country in days or hours by truck, train, and plane. First-class mail usually moves from New York City to Los Angeles in three days or less. If your letter or package is urgent, the U.S. Postal Service offers Priority Mail and Express Mail services. Priority Mail is guaranteed to go anywhere in the United States in two days or less. Express Mail will get your package there overnight.

12. Who or what is this passage about?

13. How was mail transported in the past?

14. How is mail transported now?

15. How long does first-class mail take?

16. How long does Priority Mail take?

17. How long does Express Mail take?

Once again, here's how you might have marked up this passage:

then → Today's postal service is more efficient and reliable than ever before. Mail that used to take months to move by horse and foot now moves around the country ← *now*

What a long time!

in days or hours by truck, train, and plane. First-class mail usually moves from New York City to Los Angeles in three days or less. If your letter or package is

Are there other services?

urgent, the U.S. Postal Service offers Priority Mail and Express Mail services. Priority Mail is guaranteed to go anywhere in the United States in two days or less. Express Mail will get your package there overnight.

3 services listed—
First class—3 days
Priority—2 days
Express—Overnight
Fastest

You can see how marking up a text helps make it easier to understand the information a passage conveys.

12. Who or what is this passage about? *The U.S. Postal Service.*

13. How was mail transported in the past? *By horse and foot.*

14. How is mail transported now? *By truck, train, and plane.*

15. How long does first-class mail take? *Three days or less.*

16. How long does Priority Mail take? *Two days or less.*

17. How long does Express Mail take? *Overnight.*

▶ Summary

Active reading is the first essential step to comprehension. Why? Because active reading forces you to really *see* what you're reading, to look closely at what's there.

Like a detective who arrives at the scene of a crime, if you look carefully and ask the right questions (who, what, when, where, how, and why), you're on your way to really comprehending what you read.

Skill Building until Next Time

Here are some suggestions for practicing the skills covered in this chapter throughout the day and even the rest of the week. Try them!

- **Mark up** everything you read throughout the day—the newspaper, a memo, a letter from a friend. Underline the key terms and ideas; circle and look up any unfamiliar words; write your reactions and questions in the margins. If possible, share these reactions with the writer and see if you can get answers to your questions.
- Develop a **"detective's eye."** Begin to notice things around you. Look at the details on people's faces; notice the architectural details of the buildings you enter. The more observant you are in daily life, the more enriched your life will be and the easier it will be to comprehend everything you read.

Finding the Main Idea

LESSON SUMMARY

A detective finds the facts to determine "whodunit" and what the motive was. A reader determines the facts not only for their own sake but also to find out why the author is writing: What's the main idea? This lesson shows you how to determine the main idea of what you read.

hen Lesson 1 talked about establishing the facts—the who, what, when, where, and how—it omitted one very important question: Why? Now you're ready to tackle that all-important question. Just as there's a motive behind every crime, there's also a "motive" behind every piece of writing.

All writing is communication: A writer writes to convey his or her thoughts to an audience, the reader: you. Just as you have something to say (a motive) when you pick up the phone to call someone, writers have something to say (a motive) when they pick up a pen or pencil to write. Where a detective might ask, "Why did the butler do it?" the reader might ask, "Why did the author write this? What idea is he or she trying to convey?" What you're really asking is, "What is the writer's main idea?"

Finding the main idea is much like finding the motive of the crime. It's the motive of the crime (the *why*) that usually determines the other factors (the *who, what, when, where,* and *how*). Similarly, in writing, the main idea also determines the *who, what, when,* and *where* the writer will write about, as well as *how* he or she will write.

▶ Subject vs. Main Idea

There's a difference between the *subject* of a piece of writing and its *main idea*. To see the difference, look again at the passage about the postal system. Don't skip over it! You read it in Lesson 1, but please read it again, and read it carefully.

Today's postal service is more efficient and reliable than ever before. Mail that used to take months to move by horse and foot now moves around the country in days or hours by truck, train, and plane. First-class mail usually moves from New York City to Los Angeles in three days or less. If your letter or package is urgent, the U.S. Postal Service offers Priority Mail and Express Mail services. Priority Mail is guaranteed to go anywhere in the United States in two days or less. Express Mail will get your package there overnight.

You might be asked on a standardized test, "What is the main idea of this reading?"

For this passage, you might be tempted to answer: "the post office."

But you'd be wrong.

This passage is *about* the post office, yes—but "the post office" is not the main idea of the passage. "The post office" is merely the *subject* of the passage (*who* or *what* the passage is about). The main idea must say something *about* this subject. The main idea of a text is usually an *assertion* about the subject. An assertion is a statement that requires evidence ("proof") to be accepted as true.

The main idea of a passage is an assertion about its subject, but it is something more: It is the idea that also holds together or controls the passage. The other sentences and ideas in the passage will all relate to that main idea and serve as "evidence" that the assertion is true. You might think of the main idea as a net that is cast over the other sentences. The main idea must be general enough to hold all of these ideas together.

Thus, the main idea of a passage is:

- An assertion about the subject
- The general idea that controls or holds together the paragraph or passage

Look at the postal service paragraph once more. You know what the subject is: "the post office." Now, see if you can determine the main idea. Read the passage again and look for the idea that makes an assertion about the postal service *and* holds together or controls the whole paragraph. Then answer the following question:

1. Which of the following sentences best summarizes the main idea of the passage?
    a. Express Mail is a good way to send urgent mail.
    b. Mail service today is more effective and dependable.
    c. First-class mail usually takes three days or less.

Because **a** is specific—it tells us *only* about Express Mail—it cannot be the main idea. It does not encompass the rest of the sentences in the paragraph—it doesn't cover Priority Mail or first-class mail. Answer **c** is also very specific. It tells us only about first class mail, so it, too, cannot be the main idea.

But **b**—"Mail service today is more effective and dependable"—*is* general enough to encompass the whole passage. And the rest of the sentences *support* the idea that this sentence asserts: Each sentence offers "proof" that the postal service today is indeed more efficient and reliable. Thus, the writer aims to tell us about the efficiency and reliability of today's postal service.

► Topic Sentences

You'll notice that in the paragraph about the postal service, the main idea is expressed clearly in the first sentence: "Today's postal service is more efficient and reliable than ever before." A sentence, such as this one, that clearly expresses the main idea of a paragraph or passage is often called a *topic sentence.*

In many cases, as in the postal service paragraph, the topic sentence is at the beginning of the paragraph. You will also frequently find it at the end. Less often, but on occasion, the topic sentence may be in the middle of the passage. Whatever the case, the topic sentence—like "Today's postal service is more efficient and reliable than ever before"—is an assertion, and it needs "proof." The proof is found in the facts and ideas that make up the rest of the passage. (Not all passages provide such a clear topic sentence that states the main idea. Less obvious passages will come up in later lessons.)

Practice in Identifying Topic Sentences

Remember that a topic sentence is a clear statement of the main idea of a passage; it must be general enough to encompass all the ideas in that passage, and it usually makes an assertion about the subject of that passage. Knowing all that, you can answer the following question even without reading a passage.

Practice 1

2. Which of the following sentences is general enough to be a topic sentence?
   a. The new health club has a great kickboxing class.
   b. Many different classes are offered by the health club.
   c. Pilates is a popular class at the health club.
   d. The yoga class is offered on Saturday mornings.

The answer is **b**, "Many different classes are offered by the health club." Answers **a**, **c**, and **d** are all specific examples of what is said in **b**, so they are not general enough to be topic sentences.

Practice 2

Now look at the following paragraph. Underline the sentence that expresses the main idea, and notice how the other sentences work to support that main idea.

Erik always played cops and robbers when he was a boy; now, he's a police officer. Suzanne always played school as a little girl; today, she is a high-school math teacher. Kara always played store; today, she owns a chain of retail clothing shops. Long before they are faced with the question, "What do you want to be when you grow up?" some lucky people know exactly what they want to do with their lives.

Which sentence did you underline? You should have underlined the *last* sentence: "Long before they are faced with that question 'What do you want to be when you grow up?' some lucky people know exactly what they want to do with their lives." This sentence is a good topic sentence; it expresses the idea that holds together the whole paragraph. The first three sentences—about Erik, Suzanne, and Kara—are *specific examples* of these lucky people. Notice that the topic sentence is found at the *end* of the paragraph.

Practice 3

Among the following eight sentences are *two* topics sentences. The other sentences are supporting sentences. Circle the two topic sentences. Then write the numbers of the supporting sentences that go with each topic sentence.

1. Finally, there is a concierge on duty 24 hours a day.

2. Some police offer duties, like writing reports, have no risk at all.

3. For example, there is a pool on the top floor.

4. Not all police duties are dangerous.

5. Others, like traffic duty, put police officers at very little risk.

6. Tenants of the luxury apartment building enjoy many amenities.

7. Still other duties, like investigating accidents, leave officers free of danger.

8. In addition, the lobby has a dry cleaner, an ATM machine, and a coffee shop.

Sentences 4 and 6 are the two topic sentences because both make an assertion about a general subject. The supporting sentences for topic sentence 4, "Not all police duties are dangerous," are sentences 2, 5, and 7. The supporting sentences for topic sentence 6, "Tenants of the luxury apartment building enjoy many amenities," are the remaining sentences 1, 3, and 8.

Here's how they look as paragraphs:

Not all police duties are dangerous. Some duties, like writing reports, have no risk at all. Others, like traffic duty, offer very little risk. Still other duties, like investigating accidents, leave officers free of danger.

Tenants of the luxury apartment building enjoy many amenities. For example, there is a pool on the top floor. In addition, the lobby has a dry cleaner, an ATM machine, and a coffee shop. Finally, there is a concierge on duty 24 hours a day.

You might have noticed the supporting sentences in the first paragraph about police duties begin with the following words: *some, others,* and *still other.* These words are often used to introduce examples. The second paragraph uses different words, but they have the same function: *for example, in addition,* and *finally.* If a sentence begins with such a word or phrase, that is a good indication it is *not* a topic sentence—because it is providing a specific example.

Here are some words and phrases often used to introduce specific examples:

For example	In particular
For instance	Some
In addition	Others
Furthermore	

If you're having trouble finding the main idea of a paragraph, you might try eliminating the sentences that you know contain supporting evidence.

▶ Summary

Now you can answer the last question—the *why*. What is the writer's motive? What's the main idea he or she wants to convey? By finding the sentence that makes an assertion about the subject of the paragraph and that encompasses the other sentences in the paragraph, you can uncover the author's motive.

Skill Building until Next Time

- A paragraph, by definition, is a group of sentences about the same idea. As you read today and the rest of the week, notice how texts are divided into paragraphs. What idea holds each paragraph together? Can you identify any **topic sentences**?

- Formulate **topic sentences** about things that you come across in your day. Make assertions about these people, places, and things. For example, you may eat in the cafeteria every day. Make an *assertion* about it: "This cafeteria needs remodeling," for example. Or, make an assertion about a coworker: "June is a very hard worker," you might say. Then, support your assertions. What "evidence" could you supply for your paragraph? Why do you say the cafeteria needs remodeling? Is there paint peeling off the walls? Is it still decorated 60s style? Is it not wheelchair accessible? What evidence do you have that June is a hard worker? Is she always at her computer? Does she ask informed questions in staff meetings? Does she look like she needs more sleep?

 3 ▶ Defining Vocabulary in Context

LESSON SUMMARY

An active reader looks up unfamiliar words. But what if you don't have a dictionary? In a testing situation (or, for that matter, if you're reading on the bus), you almost certainly won't be able to look up words you don't know. Instead, you can use the context to help you determine the meaning.

Sometimes in your reading, you come across words or phrases that are unfamiliar to you. You might be lucky and have a dictionary handy to look up that word or phrase, but what if you don't? How can you understand what you're reading if you don't know what all of the words mean? The answer is that you can use the rest of the passage, the *context*, to help you understand the new words.

▶ Finding Meaning from Context

The following paragraph is about one of our nation's favorite pastimes, reality TV. Read it carefully, marking it up as you go—but do NOT look up any unfamiliar words or phrases in a dictionary.

> Most reality TV shows center on two common motivators: fame and money. The shows transform waitresses, hairdressers, investment bankers, counselors, and teachers, to name a few, from obscure figures to household names. A lucky few successfully parlay their 15 minutes of fame into celebrity. Even if you are not interested in fame, you can probably understand the desire for lots of money. Watching people eat large insects, reveal their innermost thoughts to millions of people, and allow themselves to be filmed 24 hours a day for a huge financial reward makes for interesting viewing. Whatever their attraction, these shows are among the most popular on television, and every season, they proliferate like weeds in an untended garden. The networks are quickly replacing more traditional dramas and comedies with reality TV programs, which earn millions in advertising revenue. Whether you love it or hate it, one thing is for sure—reality TV is here to stay!

As you read, you may have circled some words that are unfamiliar. Did you circle *obscure* and *proliferate*? If so, don't look them up in a dictionary yet. If you do a little detective work, you can determine their definitions by looking carefully at how they are used in the paragraph.

What Does *Obscure* Mean?

Start with *obscure*. How is this word used?

> The shows transform waitresses, hairdressers, investment bankers, counselors, and teachers, to name a few, from *obscure* figures to household names.

Even if you have no idea what *obscure* means, you can still learn about the word by how it is used, by examining the words and ideas surrounding it. This is called determining word meaning through *context*. Like detectives looking for clues at a crime scene, we must look at the passage for clues that will help us define this word.

So, given the sentence we have here, what can we tell about *obscure*? Well, since the shows transform waitresses, hairdressers, investment bankers, counselors, and teachers from one position—*obscure* figures, to another position—household names, that immediately tells us that an *obscure* figure and a household name are two different things.

Furthermore, we know from the sentence that the people in question are involved in typical, everyday jobs (waitresses, hairdressers, bankers, etc.) and that from this position, they are transformed into household names, which means they achieve some level of fame and notoriety. Now you can take a pretty good guess at the meaning of *obscure*.

1. Before they become household names, the waitresses, hairdressers, investment bankers, counselors, and teachers are
   a. famous and notorious.
   b. unknown and undistinguished.
   c. unique and distinctive.

The correct answer, of course, is **b**. It certainly can't be **a**, because we know that these people are not yet famous. The reality shows will make them famous, but until that happens, they remain *obscure*. Answer **c** doesn't really make sense because we know from the passage that these people are waitresses, hairdressers, investment bankers, counselors, and teachers. Now, these are all very respectable jobs, but they are fairly common, so they wouldn't be described as unique or distinctive. Furthermore, we can tell that **b** is the correct answer because we can substitute the word obscure with the word *unknown* or *undistinguished* in the sentence and both would make sense.

Review: Finding Facts

Here's a quick review of what you learned in Lesson 1. Reality TV has the ability to take ordinary people and make them famous. However, another reason people participate in reality TV shows is

2. a. for money.
   b. because they feel lucky.
   c. because they are bored.

A quick check of the facts in the paragraph will tell you the answer is **a**, for money.

What Does *Proliferate* Mean?

Look again at the sentence in the passage in which *proliferate* is used:

Whatever their attraction, these shows are among the most popular on television, and every season, they *proliferate* like weeds in an untended garden.

Again, even if you have no idea what *proliferate* means, you can still tell what kind of word it is by the way it is used. You know, for example, that these shows proliferate like weeds in an untended garden. Therefore, you can answer this question:

3. Proliferate is a word associated with
   a. growth.
   b. reduction.
   c. disappearance.

The answer, of course, is growth. How can you tell? Well, we all know that weeds have a tendency to grow wherever they can.

Now that you've established that *proliferate* relates to growth, you can determine a more specific meaning by looking for more clues in the sentence. The sentence doesn't only tell us that these shows *proliferate* like weeds. It also tells us that they *proliferate* like weeds in an untended garden. Just imagine a neglected garden, one that has been left to its own devices. Weeds will begin to grow in every nook and cranny of that garden. In fact, they'll quickly take over, to the detriment of the plants. The phrase "weeds in an untended garden" is quite descriptive, and as such, it serves as a wonderful clue. Based on the words and phrases surrounding it, an active reader should have no problem determining the meaning of the word *proliferate*.

4. *Proliferate* in this passage means
   a. decrease, shrink.
   b. underestimate, play down.
   c. increase, spread at a rapid rate.
   d. fail, fall short.

The correct answer, of course, is **c**, "increase, spread at a rapid rate." It can't be **a** or **d** because these are things associated with reduction, not growth. And everyone knows that weeds in an untended garden will grow fast and aggressively. And **b** is not an appropriate answer because if you replace *proliferate* with underestimate or play down, it doesn't really make sense. In addition, you can tell that **c** is the right answer because the rest of the passage provides other clues. It tells you that reality TV shows are replacing other network programs, it tells you that they are popular, and it tells you that they are earning millions of dollars in advertising revenue. All these clues would indicate that reality TV shows are spreading and growing in number, not shrinking or declining. Hence, the meaning of *proliferate* must be **c**, "increase, spread at a rapid rate."

▶ How Much Context Do You Need?

In the previous example, you would still be able to understand the main message of the passage even if you didn't know—or couldn't figure out—the meaning of *obscure* and *proliferate*. In some cases, however, your understanding of a passage depends on your understanding of a particular word or phrase. Can you understand the following sentence, for example, without knowing what *adversely* means?

Reality TV shows will *adversely* affect traditional dramas and comedies.

What does *adversely* mean in this sentence? Is it something good or bad? As good a detective as you may be, there simply aren't enough clues in this sentence to tell you what this word means. But a passage with more information will give you what you need to determine meaning from context.

Reality TV shows will *adversely* affect traditional dramas and comedies. As reality TV increases in popularity, network executives will begin canceling more traditional dramas and comedies and replacing them with the latest in reality TV.

5. In the passage, *adversely* most nearly means
   a. mildly, slightly.
   b. kindly, gently.
   c. negatively, unfavorably.
   d. immediately, swiftly.

The correct answer is **c**, "negatively, unfavorably." The passage provides clues that allow you to determine the meaning of *adversely*. It tells you that as reality TV becomes more popular, network executives will cancel more traditional dramas and comedies and replace them with reality TV programming. So the meaning of adversely is neither **a**, "mild or slight," nor **b**, "kindly or gently." And based on the passage, you can't really tell if these changes will be immediate or swift (**d**) because the sentence doesn't say anything about the exact time frame in which these changes will occur. Remember, good detectives don't make assumptions they can't support with facts; and there are no facts in this sentence to support the assumption that changes will occur immediately. Thus, **c** is the best answer.

You may also have noticed that ***adversely*** is very similar to ***adversary***. And if you know that an *adversary* is a hostile opponent or enemy, then you know that *adversely* cannot be something positive. Or, if you know the word ***adversity***—hardship or misfortune—then you know that *adversely* must mean something negative or difficult. All these words share the same root—*advers*. Only the endings change.

Practice

Read the following passages and determine the meaning of the words from their context. The answers appear immediately after the questions.

Although social work is not a particularly *lucrative* career, I wouldn't do anything else. Knowing I'm helping others is far more important to me than money.

6. *Lucrative* means.
   a. highly profitable.
   b. highly rewarding.
   c. highly exciting.

When you are in an interview, try not to show any *overt* signs that you are nervous. Don't shift in your chair, shake, or stutter.

7. *Overt* means.
   a. embarrassing, awkward.
   b. subtle, suggestive.
   c. obvious, not hidden.

By the time our staff meeting ended at 8:00, I was *ravenous*. I had skipped lunch and hadn't eaten since breakfast.

8. *Ravenous* means
   a. like a raven, bird-like.
   b. extremely hungry, greedy for food.
   c. exhausted, ready for bed.

Answers

6. a. The writer says money is not important to him. If money is not an issue, it is okay that social work is not *highly profitable*, that it doesn't earn a lot of money.

7. c. Shifting, shaking, and stuttering are all *obvious, not hidden* signs of nervousness. They are not **b,** subtle or suggestive; and though they may make the interviewee feel **a,** embarrassed or awkward, the signs themselves are not embarrassing or awkward.

8. b. Because the writer hadn't eaten since breakfast, she is *extremely hungry, greedy for food*. She may also be **c,** exhausted, but the context tells us that this word has something to do with eating.

▶ Summary

The ability to determine the meaning of unfamiliar words from their context is an essential skill for reading comprehension. Sometimes, there will be unfamiliar words whose meaning you can't determine without a dictionary. But more often than not, a careful look at the context will give you enough clues to meaning.

Skill Building until Next Time

- Circle any unfamiliar words you come across today and the rest of the week. Instead of looking them up in a dictionary, try to figure out the meanings of these words from their context. Then, look them up in a dictionary to make sure you are correct.

- Begin a vocabulary list of the words you look up as you work your way through this book. Many people feel insecure about their reading and writing skills because they have a limited vocabulary. The more words you know, the easier it will be to understand what others are saying and to express what you have to say. By writing down these new words, you'll help seal them in your memory.

The Difference between Fact and Opinion

LESSON SUMMARY

To make sense of what you read, you must be able to tell whether you're reading fact or opinion. This lesson tells you how to distinguish what someone knows for certain from what someone believes.

What's the difference between fact and opinion, and what does it matter, anyway? It matters a great deal, especially when it comes to reading comprehension.

During your life, you'll be exposed to a wide variety of literature, ranging from analytical articles based on cold hard facts to fictional novels that arise wholly from the author's imagination. However, much of what you read will be a mixture of facts and the author's opinions. Part of becoming a critical reader means realizing that opinions are not evidence; for opinions to be valid, they must be supported by cold, hard facts.

Facts are:

- Things *known* for certain to have happened
- Things *known* for certain to be true
- Things *known* for certain to exist

Opinions, on the other hand, are:

- Things *believed* to have happened
- Things *believed* to be true
- Things *believed* to exist

As you can see, the key difference between fact and opinion lies in the difference between *believing* and *knowing*. Opinions may be based on facts, but they are still what we *think*, not what we *know*. Opinions are debatable; facts are not.

▶ Using Facts to Support Opinions

Reasonable opinions are those *based on fact*; and indeed, that is what much of writing is: the writer's opinion (an assertion about his or her subject) supported by facts or other evidence.

Think about the topic sentences you formed after you finished Lesson 2. Perhaps you made an assertion like this:

James is a terrific boss.

This sentence is a good topic sentence; it's an assertion about the subject, James. And it is also an opinion. It is, after all, debatable; someone could just as easily take the opposite position and say:

James is a terrible boss.

This is another good topic sentence, and it's another opinion. Now, a good writer will show his or her readers that this opinion is *valid* by supporting it with facts. For example:

James is a terrific boss. He always asks us how we're doing. He lets us leave early or come in late when we have to take care of our children. He always gives holiday bonuses. And he offers tuition reimbursement for any course, even if it has nothing to do with our position.

Notice how the topic sentence states an opinion, whereas the rest of the sentences support that opinion with facts about how James treats his employees. Now that paragraph is much more effective than something like this:

James is a terrible boss. I really don't like him. He just can't get along with people. And he has stupid ideas about politics.

Why is the first paragraph so much better? Because it's not just opinion. It's opinion supported by evidence. The second paragraph is all opinion. Every sentence is debatable; every sentence tells us what the author *believes* is true, but not what is *known* to be true. The author of the second paragraph doesn't provide any evidence to support why he or she thinks that James is such a lousy boss. As a result, we're not likely to take his or her opinion very seriously.

In the first paragraph, on the other hand, the writer offers concrete evidence for why he or she *believes* James is a great boss. After the initial opinion, the writer provides facts—specific things James does (which can be verified by other observers) that make him a good boss. You may still not agree that James is a great boss, but at least you can see exactly why this writer thinks so.

▶ Distinguishing Fact from Opinion

When you read academic materials, very often you will have to distinguish between fact and opinion—between what the writer thinks and how the writer supports what he or she thinks, between what is proven to be true and what needs to be proved.

A good test for whether something is a fact or opinion might be to ask yourself, "Can this statement be debated? Is this known for certain to be true?" If you answer *yes* to the first question, you have an opinion; if you answer *yes* to the second, you have a fact.

Practice 1

Try these questions on the following statements. Read them carefully, and then write F in the blank if the statement is a fact and O if it is an opinion. The answers appear right after the questions.

_____ **1.** The Academy Awards honor the film industry.

_____ **2.** The Academy Awards are always fun to watch.

_____ **3.** More independent films should win Academy Awards.

_____ **4.** The Academy Awards are an annual event.

_____ **5.** Best director is the most interesting Academy Award category.

Answers

1. Fact

2. Opinion

3. Opinion

4. Fact

5. Opinion

Practice 2

Now try the same exercise with a complete paragraph. Underline the facts and use a highlighter or colored pen to highlight the opinions. Be careful—you may find fact and opinion together in the same sentence. When you've finished, you can check your answers against the marked passage that follows.

There are many different ways to invest your money to provide for a financially secure future. Many people invest in stocks and bonds, but I think good old-fashioned savings accounts and CDs (certificates of deposit) are the best way to invest your hard-earned money. Stocks and bonds are often risky, and it doesn't make sense to risk losing the money you've worked so hard for. True, regular savings accounts and CDs can't make you a millionaire overnight or provide the high returns some stock investments do. But by the same token, savings accounts and CDs are fully insured and provide steady, secure interest on your money. That makes a whole lot of cents.

Answers

How did you do? Was it easy to distinguish between the facts and the opinions? Here's what your marked-up passage should look like. The facts are underlined and the opinions are in boldface type.

> There are many different ways to invest your money to provide for a financially secure future. Many people invest in stocks and bonds, **but I think good old-fashioned savings accounts and CDs (certificates of deposit) are the best way to invest your hard-earned money.** Stocks and bonds are often risky, **and it doesn't make sense to risk losing the money you've worked so hard for.** True, regular savings accounts and CDs can't make you a millionaire overnight or provide the high returns some stock investments do. But by the same token, savings accounts and CDs are fully insured and provide steady, secure interest on your money. **That makes a whole lot of cents.**

Practice 3

To strengthen your ability to distinguish between fact and opinion, try this. Take a fact, such as:

FACT: *Wednesday is the fourth day of the week.*

Now, turn it into an opinion. Make it something debatable, like this:

OPINION: *Wednesday is the longest day of the week.*

Here's another example.

FACT: *You must be 18 years old to vote in the United States.*

OPINION: *The voting age should be lowered to 16 years of age.*

Now you try. Suggested answers come after the questions.

6. FACT: *Healthcare costs have risen over the last several years.*

OPINION:

7. FACT: *The 22nd Amendment of the United States Constitution establishes a two-term limit for the presidency.*

OPINION:

8. FACT: *More than 58,000 Americans lost their lives in the Vietnam War.*

OPINION:

9. FACT: *The Motion Picture Association R (Restricted) rating requires anyone under 17 to be accompanied by a parent or adult guardian.*

OPINION:

10. FACT: *Use of performance-enhancing drugs is strictly prohibited in both amateur and professional sports.*

OPINION:

Answers

There are, of course, many opinions you could form from these subjects. Here are some possible answers.

6. Our government should make healthcare a higher priority.
Companies should give employees several healthcare programs from which to choose.
People should stop complaining about healthcare costs.
7. Presidents should be allowed to serve for three terms.
Limiting service to two terms will make U.S. presidents more effective.
Term limits are a very bad idea.

8. American soldiers should not have been sent to Vietnam.
Our government did all the right things concerning the Vietnam War.
9. The Motion Picture Association should not be able to rate films.
The Motion Picture Association ratings should be taken seriously by all parents.
Movie ratings are useless.
10. Performance-enhancing drugs should be legal.
Competitive sports would be more interesting to watch if performance-enhancing drugs were legal.
Performance-enhancing drugs are the worst thing that ever happened to competitive sports.

▶ Summary

The ability to differentiate between fact and opinion is a very important skill. Like a detective, you need to know the difference between what people *think* and what people *know*, between what people *believe* to be true and what has been *proven* to be true. Then you will be able to see whether writers support their opinions, and if they do, how they do it. This will allow you to judge for yourself the validity of those opinions.

Skill Building until Next Time

- Listen carefully to what people say today and try to determine whether they are stating a fact or expressing an opinion. When they offer opinions, do they support them?
- As you come across facts and opinions today, practice turning them into their opposites; make facts out of opinions and opinions out of facts.

 Putting It All Together

LESSON SUMMARY

This lesson reviews what you learned in Lessons 1–4: getting the facts, finding the main idea, determining what words mean in context, and distinguishing between fact and opinion. In this lesson, you'll get vital practice in using all four skills at once.

In order to solve a crime, a detective cannot *just* get the facts of the case, *just* discover the motive, *just* decipher difficult clues, or *just* distinguish between fact and opinion. To be successful, a detective must do all these things at the same time. Similarly, reading really can't be broken down into these separate tasks. Reading comprehension comes from employing all these strategies simultaneously. This lesson gives you the opportunity to combine these strategies and take your reading comprehension skills to the next level.

▶ Review: What You've Learned so Far

These are the strategies you studied in the past four lessons:

- **Lesson 1: Find the facts in what you read.** You practiced looking for the basic information that was being conveyed in the paragraphs: the who, what, when, where, and how.
- **Lesson 2: Find the main idea.** You learned about topic sentences and how they express an assertion about the subject of the paragraph. You saw how the main idea must be general enough to encompass all other sentences in the paragraph; it is the thought that controls the paragraph, and the other sentences work to support that main idea.
- **Lesson 3: Determine the meaning of words from context.** You practiced looking for clues to determine meaning in the words and sentences surrounding the unfamiliar word or phrase.
- **Lesson 4: Distinguish between fact and opinion.** You learned that a fact is something *known* to be true, whereas an opinion is something *believed* to

be true. You practiced distinguishing between the two and saw how good paragraphs use facts to support opinions.

> **If any of these terms or strategies sound unfamiliar to you, STOP. Take a few minutes to review whatever lesson is unclear.**

▶ Practice

In this lesson, you will sharpen your reading comprehension skills by using all of these strategies at once. This will become more natural to you as your reading skills develop.

Practice Passage 1

Begin by looking at the following paragraph. Remember to read actively; mark up the text as you go. Then answer the questions on the next page. An example of how to mark up the passage, as well as the answers to the questions, follow.

It is clear that the United States is a nation that needs to eat healthier and slim down. One of the most important steps in the right direction would be for school cafeterias to provide healthy, low-fat options for students. In every town and city, an abundance of fast-food restaurants lure teenage customers with fast, inexpensive, and tasty food, but these foods are typically unhealthy. Unfortunately, school cafeterias—in an effort to provide food that is appetizing to young people—mimic fast food menus, often serving items such as burgers and fries, pizza, hot dogs, and fried chicken. While these foods do provide some nutritional value, they are relatively high in fat. Many of the lunch selections school cafeterias currently offer could be made healthier with a few simple and inexpensive substitutions. Veggie burgers, for example, offered alongside beef burgers, would be a positive addition. A salad bar would also serve the purpose of providing a healthy and satisfying meal. And tasty grilled chicken sandwiches would be a far better option than fried chicken. Additionally, the beverage case should be stocked with containers of low-fat milk.

1. What is the subject of this passage?

2. According to the passage, which of the following options would make healthy, low-fat additions to a school cafeteria's offerings? (Circle all correct answers.)
  a. tofu
  b. veggie burgers
  c. low-fat milk
  d. fries
  e. salad bar
  f. grilled chicken sandwiches
  g. stir-fried vegetables

3. The meaning of *mimic* is
  a. reject.
  b. copy.
  c. ignore.
  d. disregard.

4. Which of the following best summarizes the main idea of the passage?
  a. Teenagers love to eat fast food more than anything else.
  b. School cafeterias should serve veggie burgers.
  c. School cafeterias should be providing healthy, low-fat options for students.

5. True or False: "One of the most important steps in the right direction would be for school cafeterias to provide healthy, low-fat options for students" is a topic sentence.

6. True or False: "One of the most important steps in the right direction would be for school cafeterias to provide healthy, low-fat options for students" is an opinion.

Marking Practice Passage 1

Before you check the answers, look again at the paragraph. Did you mark it up? If so, it may look something like this:

It is clear that the United States is a nation that needs to eat healthier and slim down. <u>One of the most important steps in the right direction would be for school cafeterias to provide healthy, low-fat options for students.</u> *main idea* In every town and city, an abundance of fast-food restaurants lure teenage customers with fast, inexpensive, and tasty food, but these foods are typically unhealthy. Unfortunately, school cafeterias—in an effort to provide food that is appetizing to young people—*to copy* (mimic) fast food menus, often serving items such as <u>burgers and fries, *high-fat lunch offerings* pizza, hot dogs, and fried chicken</u>. While these foods do provide some nutritional value, they are relatively high in fat. Many of the lunch selections school cafeterias currently offer could be made healthier with a few simple and inexpensive substitutions. <u>Veggie burgers</u>, *possible healthy low-fat lunch options* for example, offered alongside beef burgers, would be a positive addition. <u>A salad bar</u> would also serve the purpose of providing a healthy and satisfying meal. And <u>tasty grilled chicken sandwiches</u> would be a far better option than fried chicken. Additionally, the beverage case should be stocked with containers of <u>low-fat milk</u>.

Answers

1. The subject of the passage is *healthier, low-fat lunch options in school cafeterias*. Remember, the subject of a passage is who or what the passage is about.

2. b, c, e, f. These results are all mentioned in the passage. Tofu (**a**) and stir-fried vegetables (**g**) are both healthy, low-fat lunch options, but they are not mentioned *in the passage*. Fries (**d**) are mentioned, but they are not low-fat and are mentioned as one of the unhealthy items that should be replaced.

Remember, you're looking for the facts that the *author* has provided. It is extremely important, especially in test situations, not to put in an answer that isn't in the text. Logic may tell you that tofu and stir-fried vegetables are healthy, low-fat lunch options, but the paragraph doesn't tell you this. You need to stick to the facts. Any assumption that you make about a passage must be grounded in evidence found in that passage itself.

3. b. *Mimic* means to copy. The most obvious clue is the way the word is used in the sentence. "*Unfortunately, school cafeterias—in an effort to provide food that is appetizing to young people—mimic fast food menus, often serving items such as burgers and fries, pizza, hot dogs, and fried chicken.*" Burgers and fries, pizza, hot dogs, and fried chicken are all foods served by fast-food restaurants, and if school cafeterias are also serving those foods, they are clearly *copying* fast-food menus, not *rejecting*, *ignoring*, or *disregarding* them.

4. c. Answer **a** is an assumption not based on anything written in the passage. Answer **b** is too specific—it is only one example of a healthy, low-fat lunch option that a school cafeteria can serve. Only **c** is general and factual enough to encompass the whole paragraph.

5. True. This sentence expresses the main idea.

6. True. This sentence is an opinion. It is debatable. Someone else might think that altering the menu in school cafeterias isn't one of the most important steps to be taken in order to make the United States a healthier, slimmer nation. They might think that launching a public service ad campaign about the dangers of fast food or implementing more rigorous classroom education about eating healthy is more important than changing the menus of school cafeterias.

How did you do? If you got all six answers correct, congratulations! If you missed one or more questions, check the following table to see which lessons to review.

IF YOU MISSED:	THEN STUDY:
Question 1	Lesson 2
Question 2	Lesson 1
Question 3	Lesson 3
Question 4	Lesson 2
Question 5	Lesson 2
Question 6	Lesson 4

Practice Passage 2

Try one more paragraph to conclude this first section. Once again, mark up the paragraph carefully and then answer the questions that follow.

Robert Johnson is the best blues guitarist of all time. There is little information available about this legendary blues guitarist, and the information is as much rumor as fact. What is indisputable, however, is Johnson's tremendous impact on the world of rock and roll. Some consider Johnson the father of modern rock: His influence extends to artists from Muddy Waters to Led Zeppelin, from the Rolling Stones to the Allman Brothers Band. Eric Clapton has called Johnson the most important blues musician who ever lived. Considering his reputation, it is hard to believe that Johnson recorded only 29 songs before his death in 1938, purportedly at the hands of a jealous husband. He was only 27 years old, yet he left an indelible mark on the music world. Again and again, contemporary rock artists return to Johnson, whose songs capture the very essence of the blues, transforming our pain and suffering with the healing magic of his guitar. Rock music wouldn't be what it is today without Robert Johnson.

7. According to the passage, from what musical tradition did Robert Johnson emerge?
   a. rock and roll
   b. jazz
   c. blues

8. Johnson died in
   a. 1927.
   b. 1938.
   c. 1929.

9. True or False: Johnson influenced many rock artists, including Led Zeppelin and the Rolling Stones.

10. Johnson's cause of death was
   a. heart attack.
   b. old age.
   c. murder.

11. *Indelible* means
   a. permanent, impossible to remove.
   b. fleeting, brief.
   c. troubling, disturbing.

12. The main idea of this paragraph is best expressed in which sentence in the paragraph?

13. Indicate whether the following sentences are *fact* or *opinion*:
   a. "Robert Johnson is the best blues guitarist of all time."
   b. "Eric Clapton has called Johnson the most important blues musician who ever lived."
   c. "Rock music wouldn't be what it is today without Robert Johnson."

Answers

7. c. See the first and second sentences. The next-to-last sentence also provides this information.

8. b. See the sixth sentence.

9. True. See the fourth sentence.

10. c. See the sixth sentence.

11. a. *permanent, impossible to remove.* There are several context clues. The third, fourth, and fifth sentences discuss Johnson's major impact on musicians who have followed him. The next-to-last sentence also discusses the fact that contemporary artists return to Johnson again and again. Also, the sentence that uses the word *indelible* states, "He was only 27 years old, yet he left an indelible mark on the music world," implying that he left a lasting mark in spite of his young age. These clues make it obvious that (**b**) fleeting, brief and (**c**) troubling, disturbing are not the correct answers.

12. The third sentence. The point of the whole passage, which is Johnson's impact on rock and roll, is very clearly stated in the third sentence, "What is indisputable, however, is Johnson's tremendous impact on the world of rock and roll."

13. Choice **a** is **opinion**. It is debatable whether Johnson is the best blues guitarist of all time.
Choice **b** is **fact**. This is verifiable information.
Choice **c** is **opinion** because this is a debatable proposition.

How did you do this time? Better? If you missed any questions, this time, *you* figure out which questions correspond with which lessons. This will help you see with what categories you most need help.

Skill Building until Next Time

- Review the Skill Building sections from each lesson this week. Try any Skill Builders you haven't attempted.
- Write a paragraph about what you've learned in this section. Begin your paragraph with a clear topic sentence, like: "I've learned several reading strategies since Lesson 1" or "I've learned that reading comprehension isn't as difficult as I thought." Then, write several sentences that support or explain your assertion. Try to use at least one vocabulary word that you've learned in this section.

▶ Structure

ow that you've covered the basics, you can begin to focus on one specific reading comprehension strategy: structure. How do writers organize their ideas?

You might want to think of a writer as an architect. Every building has a number of rooms. But how these rooms are arranged is up to the architect. The same goes for a piece of writing—how the sentences and ideas are arranged is entirely up to the writer. However, most architects—and most writers—generally follow certain patterns, not because they can't think on their own, but because these patterns work. In this section, you'll study four organizational patterns that work for writers:

1. Chronological order
2. Order of importance
3. Compare and contrast
4. Cause and effect

You'll learn to recognize these patterns and some of the reasons why writers use them.

6 ▶ Start from the Beginning: Chronological Order

LESSON SUMMARY

This lesson focuses on one of the simplest structures writers use: chronological order, or arrangement of events by the order in which they occured.

There are many ways to tell a story. Some stories start in the middle and flash backward to the beginning; a few start at the end and tell the story in reverse. But most of the time, stories start at the beginning. Writers often begin with what happened first and then tell what happened next, and next, and so on, until the end. When writers tell a story in this order, from beginning to end in the order in which things happened, they are telling it in *chronological* order. *Chronology* is the arrangement of events in the order in which they occurred.

► Chronology and Transitions

Much of what you read is arranged in chronological order. Newspaper and magazine articles, minutes of meetings, explanations of procedures, and so on are usually arranged this way. For example, look at the following paragraph that might be found in a company newsletter:

This year's employee award ceremony was a tremendous success. The first award was given to Carlos Fe for Perfect Attendance. The second award, for Most Dedicated Employee, went to Jennifer Steele. Then, our president, Martin Lucas, interrupted the awards ceremony to announce that he and his wife were having a baby. When he finished, everyone stood up for a congratulatory toast. Afterward, the third award was given to Karen Hunt for Most Inspiring Employee. Finally, President Lucas ended the ceremony by giving everyone a bonus check for $100.

You'll notice that this paragraph tells what happened at the ceremony from start to finish. You'll also notice that you can tell the order in which things happened in two ways. First, you can tell by the order of the sentences themselves—first things first, last things last. Second, you can tell by the use of *transitional words and phrases*, which signal a shift from one idea to the next. Here is the same paragraph with the transitional words underlined:

This year's employee award ceremony was a tremendous success. The <u>first</u> award was given to Carlos Fe for Perfect Attendance. The <u>second</u> award, for Most Dedicated Employee, went to Jennifer Steele. <u>Then</u>, our president, Martin Lucas, interrupted the awards ceremony to announce that he and his wife were having a baby. <u>When</u> he finished, everyone stood up for a congratulatory toast. <u>Afterward</u>, the <u>third</u> award was given to Karen Hunt for Most Inspiring

Employee. <u>Finally</u>, President Lucas ended the ceremony by giving everyone a bonus check for $100.

The underlined words—*first, second, then, when, afterward, third*, and *finally*—are transitional words that keep these events linked together in chronological order. Look at how the paragraph sounds without these words:

This year's employee award ceremony was a tremendous success. The award was given to Carlos Fe for Perfect Attendance. The award for Most Dedicated Employee went to Jennifer Steele. Our president, Martin Lucas, interrupted the awards ceremony to announce that he and his wife were having a baby. He finished; everyone stood up for a congratulatory toast. The award was given to Karen Hunt for Most Inspiring Employee. President Lucas ended the ceremony by giving everyone a bonus check for $100.

It doesn't sound quite as good, does it?

► Practice with Transitional Words and Phrases

Practice Passage 1

Here's a more extreme example of a paragraph with the transitional words and phrases omitted:

I went to work early to get some extra filing done. I got there; the phone started ringing. My boss walked in. He asked me to type a letter for him. He asked me to make arrangements for a client to stay in town overnight. I looked at my watch; it was already 11:00.

Now, take the paragraph and add the following transitional words and phrases:

immediately	yesterday
as soon as	a moment later
when	then

_____ I went to work early to get some extra filing done. _____ I got there, the phone started ringing. _____ my boss walked in. _____ he asked me to type a letter for him. _____ he asked me to make arrangements for a client to stay in town overnight. _____ I looked at my watch, it was already 11:00.

See how much better the paragraph sounds with transitional words and phrases to guide you?

Answers

You might have come up with a slightly different version, but here's one good way to fill in the blanks:

Yesterday, I went to work early to get some extra filing done. As soon as I got there, the phone started ringing. A moment later, my boss walked in. Immediately, he asked me to type up a letter for him. Then he asked me to make arrangements for a client to stay in town overnight. When I looked at my watch, it was already 11:00.

Practice Passage 2

Here is a series of events listed in random order. Use the transitional words and phrases in each sentence to help you put them in proper chronological order. Number the sentences from 1–6 in the blank provided.

_____ If the penalty structure is to your liking, make sure that the money market account is FDIC insured.

_____ After you've found the best terms, be sure to find out what the minimum account balance is and ask what the penalties are if your account drops below the limit.

_____ In order to open a money market account, you should follow several steps.

_____ Then you should shop around for the best terms and yields available.

_____ Finally, once the account is opened and you are earning interest, you should consider using that interest to pay off outstanding credit card debt.

_____ First, you should decide what features are important to you.

Answers

You should have numbered the blanks in this order: 5, 4, 1, 3, 6, 2. Here's how the sentences look together in a paragraph.

In order to open a money market account, you should follow several steps. First, you should decide what features are important to you. Then you should shop around for the best terms and yields available. After you've found the best terms, be sure to find out what the minimum account balance is and ask what the penalties are if your account drops below the limit. If the penalty structure is to your liking, make sure that the money market account is FDIC insured. Finally, once the account is opened and you are earning interest, you should consider using that interest to pay off outstanding credit card debt.

Practice Passage 3

Read the following paragraph, which describes a local community event.

The International Dinner raised $15,000 to renovate the Berkshire Park Community Center. Three-hundred and fifty people attended the dinner, which was held in the ballroom of a local hotel. Tickets were sold in advance for $50 each. The attendees left the event feeling very good about their community. The Berkshire Park Community Center was damaged in a fire six months ago. An energetic committee of eight community members came up with the idea of the International Dinner to raise funds to repair the damages. The plan was to celebrate the diversity of the Berkshire Park Neighborhood Association by serving ethnic food that represents the various cultures in the neighborhood. The committee also organized a silent auction with prizes donated by local businesses to take place during the dinner. The committee chairperson talked to a local newspaper reporter at the dinner and stated that the goal was to raise $10,000. A follow-up letter to community members thanked everyone for the huge success of the fundraiser and outlined a schedule for the renovation.

Notice that this paragraph is not arranged in chronological order. Take the ten different events that make up the story and rearrange them so that they are in chronological order.

Here's the order of events as they are presented in the story.

- The International Dinner raised $15,000 to renovate the Berkshire Park Community Center.
- Three-hundred and fifty people attended the dinner.
- Tickets were sold for $50 each.
- The attendees left the event feeling very good about their community.

- The Community Center was damaged in a fire six months ago.
- A committee of eight community members came up with the idea of the International Dinner to raise funds for repairs.
- The plan was to serve foods that represent the various cultures in the neighborhood.
- The committee organized a silent auction to take place during the dinner.
- The chairperson talked to a local newspaper reporter stating the goal was to raise $10,000.
- A letter to community members thanked everyone and outlined the schedule for renovation.

Now put the events in chronological order.

1.

2.

3.

4.

5.

6.

7.

8.

9.

10.

Now, take these chronologically ordered events and make them into a cohesive paragraph. To do this, you need to add transitional words and phrases. Here is a list of transitional words and phrases often used in chronologically organized passages:

first	soon
second	after
third	before
next	during
now	while
then	meanwhile
when	in the meantime
as soon as	at last
immediately	eventually
suddenly	finally

Write your paragraph, putting the events in chronological order with transitional phrases, below or on a separate piece of paper.

Answers

There are, of course, many possible ways of using transitional words and phrases to put this story in chronological order. One paragraph might look like this:

The Berkshire Park Community Center was damaged in a fire six months ago. <u>Soon after</u>, a committee of eight community members came up with the idea of an International Dinner to raise funds to repair the damages. The plan was to serve foods that represent the various cultures in the neighborhood. <u>In addition</u>, the committee organized a silent auction to take place during the dinner. <u>Before</u> the event, tickets were sold for $50 each. <u>During</u> the dinner, the committee chairperson talked to a local newspaper reported and stated that the goal was to raise $10,000. Three-hundred and fifty people attended the event which raised $15,000. <u>When</u> the attendees left the event, they felt very good about their community. <u>After</u> the event, a letter was sent to community members thanking them for everything <u>while</u> outlining a schedule for renovation.

Practice Passage 4

Chronological order is very important, especially when it comes to procedures. If you perform the steps out of chronological order, you won't get the results you desire. Just imagine, for example, that you are trying to bake a cake. What happens when you do things out of order? You go without dessert.

Of course, the consequences of not following proper chronological order at work can be much more serious, so it's important that you strengthen this skill. Read the following paragraph, marking it up to help you keep track of the steps that an employee must follow to get tuition reimbursement.

Our company will be happy to reimburse you for college courses that enhance your job performance. Before you register for the course, you must get approval first from your immediate supervisor and then from Human Resources. If you are taking the course for credit, you must receive a C+ or better in the course. If you are not taking it for credit, you must pass the course. After you have completed the course, you must write a report explaining the content of the course and its relevance to your position. Then, you must fill out a reimbursement request. Attach a tuition payment receipt, your report, and a copy of your grades to this request and promptly submit this request to your supervisor. Once your supervisor has approved the request, you can then submit all these forms to Human Resources, and you should receive your check within two weeks.

There are eight separate steps an employee must take to be reimbursed for college course work. What are they? List them below in the order in which the employee must do them.

1.

2.

3.

4.

5.

6.

7.

8.

If you marked up your paragraph, you should easily see the different steps. Here's how you might have marked it up. The transitional words and phrases are highlighted in bold.

Our company will be happy to reimburse you for college courses that enhance *need approval before registering!*
1 your job performance. **Before** you register for the course, you must get approval *1st —get supervisor approval*
2 **first** from your immediate supervisor and **then** from Human Resources. If you *2nd —get HR approval*
3 are taking the course for credit, you must receive a C+ or better in the course. If *3rd —take course— get C+ or better!*
4 you are not taking it for credit, you must pass the course. **After** you have com-
5 pleted the course, you must write a report explaining the content of the course *4th —write report*
6 and its relevance to your position. **Then**, you must fill out a reimburse- *5th —fill out reimb. request*
7 ment request. Attach a tuition payment receipt, your report, and a copy of your *6th —attach tuition, report + grades to request*
8 grades to this request and **promptly** submit this request to your supervisor. Once
your supervisor has approved the request, you can **then** submit all these forms to *7th —submit to supervisor*
Human Resources, and you should receive your check within two weeks. *8th —submit to HR*

If you miss a step in this process, you won't be reimbursed. Thus, it's critical that you be able to identify each step and the order in which the steps must be taken.

► Summary

Chronological structure is, of course, a very useful organizational pattern. Events happen in a certain order, so writers often present them in that order. Keep an eye out for the transitional words and phrases that signal this type of organization.

Skill Building until Next Time

- As you think about things today, try to organize them chronologically. If you think back to something that happened over the weekend, for example, think about it in the order it happened: First ____, then _____, suddenly, _____, and so on.
- As you read about events in the newspaper or in other places, put the different pieces of each event in chronological order, as you did with the story about the International Dinner.

Order of Importance

LESSON SUMMARY

Continuing your study of the structure of reading material, this lesson shows you how writers use order of importance—from least to most important or from most to least important. Understanding this commonly used structure improves your reading comprehension by helping you see what's most important in a piece of writing.

t's a scientifically proven fact: People remember most what they learn *first* and *last* in a given session. Writers have instinctively known this for a long time. That's why many pieces of writing are organized not in chronological order but *by order of importance*.

Imagine again that the writer is like an architect. How would this type of writer arrange the rooms? By hierarchy. A *hierarchy* is a group of things arranged by rank or order of importance. In this type of organizational pattern, *hierarchy*, not chronology, determines order. Thus, this architect would lay the rooms out like so: When you walk in the front door, the first room you encounter would be the president's office, then the vice president's, then the assistant vice president's, and so on down to the lowest ranking worker. Or, vice versa, the architect may choose for you to meet the least important employee first, the one with the least power in the company. Then the next, and the next, until at last, you reach the president.

Likewise, in writing, ideas may be arranged in order of importance. In this pattern, which idea comes first? Not the one that *happened* first, but the one that is *most*, or *least*, important.

► Most Important to Least Important

In the following paragraph, the writer starts with what is most important, hoping that by putting this item first, the reader will be sure to remember it. After you read the passage, answer the questions that follow. Each question is followed by its answer to guide you through your reading of the passage.

Choosing a doctor is an important decision. Here are some things you can do to make the best choice. The single most important thing is to interview the doctors you are considering. Ask questions about the practice, office hours, and how quickly he or she responds to phone calls. Pay attention to the doctor's communication skills and how comfortable you are with him or her. The second thing you should do is check the doctor's credentials. One way to do this is to ask your healthcare insurance company how they checked the doctor's credentials before accepting him or her into their network. Another thing you can do is to look at the environment of the doctor's office. Be sure patients aren't waiting too long and that the office is clean and professional. Finally, spend some time talking with the receptionist. Keep in mind that this is the person you'll come into contact with every time you call or come into the office. If he or she is pleasant and efficient, it will certainly make your overall experience better.

1. According to the passage, what's the most important thing you can do to be sure you choose the right doctor?

The answer, of course, should be clear: The writer tells you clearly that the "single most important thing is to interview the doctors you are considering."

2. What is the second most important thing you can to choose the right doctor?

When a writer starts out by saying "the most important thing," you know that the writer will be starting with the most important idea and ending with the least important. The second best thing, therefore, is the second piece of advice offered in the paragraph: "Check the doctor's credentials."

3. What's the third most important thing?

Since the writer is going from most to least important, then according the passage, the third most important thing is to "look at the environment of the doctor's office."

4. Finally, what is the *least* important tip the writer offers?

Of course, the answer is the last piece of advice the writer offers: "Spend some time talking with the receptionist."

► Least Important to Most Important

Some writers prefer the opposite approach, depending on the subject and the effect they want their writing to have. Rather than *starting* with the most important idea, they prefer to *end* with what is most important. Not only do they leave you with a strong concluding impression, but they also take advantage of the "snowball effect." The snowball effect is the "buildup" or force that a writer gets from starting with what's least important and moving toward what's most important. Like a snowball, the writer's idea builds and builds, gets bigger and bigger, more and more important. By starting with the least important point, writers can also create suspense—the reader is waiting for that final idea. And each idea or item builds upon the ones that come before it (as in a snowball).

Here's an example of a passage that builds from least important to most important. Read the passage, marking it up as you go along. Answer the questions that follow.

There are a number of reasons why the current voting age of 18 should be lowered to 16. First, a lower voting age in the United States would encourage other countries to follow this example. Many countries are discussing and debating the pros and cons of lowering the voting age, and if the United States gives 16-year-olds the right to vote, it will serve as an important example for the rest of the world.

More importantly, if 16-year-olds are old enough to engage in other adult activities, then they are old enough to vote. In many states, 16-year-olds can work, get a driver's license, and engage in many other adult activities that make them mature enough to vote. If, at 16, a young person is old enough to manage the responsibilities of work and school, then it is clear that they are responsible enough to make informed decisions about politics and politicians.

But the most important reason why the voting age should be lowered to 16 is that it will decrease apathy and cynicism while stimulating a lifelong interest in political participation. Many young people feel as though their opinion doesn't matter. By the time they reach voting age, they are often disenchanted with politics and cynical about the entire political process. If the voting age was lowered to 16, young people would know that their opinion does count. They would be inspired to exercise their right to vote not just as young adults but throughout their lives. The long-term results—a much higher percentage of interested voters and better voter turnout—will benefit our entire nation.

In the following spaces, list the reasons the author provides for why the voting age should be lowered *in the order in which they are listed in the passage.* In the next set of blanks, list those same reasons *in their order of importance.*

Order of Presentation

1.

2.

3.

Order of Importance

1.

2.

3.

You see, of course, that the orders are reversed: The author starts with what is least important and ends with what is most important. Why? Why not the other way around?

This author uses a least-to-most-important organizational strategy because he is making an argument. He's trying to convince you that the United States should lower the voting age to 16. In order to be convincing, he must have a strong argument. If he starts with what he feels is his most important (and most convincing) point, he has already shown his hand, so to speak. Especially when the issue is controversial, writers often use the least-to-most-important structure. That way, if their less important points make sense to the reader, then their more important points will come off even stronger. Also, if they were to organize their ideas in the reverse order, most to least important, readers might feel let down.

Thus, you can often expect to see this type of structure—least to most important—in an argument. As the saying goes, "save the best for last." In an argument, that's usually where "the best" has the most impact.

In the first example, about choosing a doctor, the writer was not trying to convince. She was simply giving some advice. There's no need, then, for a buildup. Indeed, in that kind of paragraph, readers might stop reading after the first tip if they don't find it helpful. That's why the most important ideas come first—to make sure they'll be read.

In other words, the writer's purpose—his or her motive for writing—influences the choice of organizational patterns. In turn, the structure influences how you take in and understand what you read.

Practice

Look at the following list of reasons to read more often. If you were to put these reasons together in a paragraph to convince readers that they should read more, how would you organize them? Rank these reasons first in order of importance and then in the order in which you would present them.

Five Reasons to Read More Often

- It will improve your vocabulary.
- It will improve your reading comprehension.
- It will increase your reading speed.
- It will broaden your understanding of yourself and others.
- It will introduce you to new information and ideas.

Order of Importance to You

1.

2.

3.

4.

5.

Order of Presentation

1.

2.

3.

4.

5.

In which order did you choose to present your ideas? Most important to least important? Or least to most? Either structure will work beautifully with these ideas. You may want to hit your readers with what's most important from the start so that you make sure you catch their attention. Or you may want to save your best idea for last so that your readers get through all the other ideas first and build up to the most important. You might present the ideas differently, but here are two versions of the resulting paragraph as examples.

Example: Most to Least Important

There are many benefits to reading more often. First and foremost, reading more will broaden your understanding of yourself and of other people. It will also introduce you to new information and ideas. Furthermore, it will improve your overall reading comprehension so you'll begin to understand more of what you read. In addition, reading more will improve your vocabulary and increase your reading speed.

Example: Least to Most Important

There are many benefits to reading more often. First, it will increase your reading speed, so that you can read more in less time. Second, it will improve your vocabulary. Third, it will improve your overall reading comprehension, and you'll understand more of what you read. In addition, reading more will introduce you to new information and ideas. Most importantly, it will broaden your understanding of yourself and of other people.

Review
Transitions
Notice how the transitional words and phrases are used in these paragraphs. Go back to each paragraph and underline the transitional words and phrases.

Here are the words you should have underlined in the first paragraph: *first and foremost, also, furthermore,* and *in addition.* The second paragraph uses different transitional words and phrases: *first, second, third, in addition,* and *most importantly.*

Main Idea
By the way, what is the main idea of the two paragraphs above? Do you see a topic sentence? Write the main idea of the paragraphs in this space.

You can probably recognize by now that the first sentence in each paragraph, "There are many benefits to reading more often," is the topic sentence that governs each paragraph. This sentence is general enough to encompass each of the different reasons given, and it makes an assertion about reading—that you should do it more often.

▶ Summary

Organizing ideas by order of importance is a structure you will see often. Whether a passage is organized from most to least important or least to most, this technique should now be easy for you to recognize.

Skill Building until Next Time

- As you come across lists today, see how they are organized. Are they organized by order of importance? If so, are the items listed from least to most important or from most to least? If the lists are not organized hierarchically, try to organize them by their order of importance.
- Create your own "order of importance" paragraph like the one on reasons to read more often. Some topics you might write about are reasons for a four-day work week, reasons why your career is best, things you need to do this week, and so forth.

Similarities and Differences: Compare and Contrast

LESSON SUMMARY

This lesson explores another organizational pattern writers often use to structure their writing: comparison and contrast.

We spend a good deal of our lives comparing and contrasting things. Whenever we want to explain something, for example, we often use *comparison* (showing how two or more things are *similar*). We might say, for example, that mint chocolate chip ice cream tastes just like a York Peppermint Pattie; or that the new manager looks just like Clint Eastwood. When we want to show how things are *different* or not alike, we **contrast** them. We might say that York Peppermint Patties are mintier than any mint chocolate chip ice cream; or that the new manager may look like Eastwood, but he doesn't have Eastwood's dimple.

▶ How Comparison and Contrast Work

When writers compare and contrast, they provide a way of classifying or judging the items they are discussing. They show how two (or more) things are similar or different when placed side by side. Consider, for example, the following paragraph. Read it carefully, and then answer the questions that follow.

Planting a garden is a lot like having a family. Both require a great deal of work, especially as they grow and as the seasons change. As summer days lengthen, your plants become dependent on you for sustenance, much like your children depend on you for food and drink. Like a thirsty child asking for a drink of water, your plants do the same. Their bent, wilted "body" language, translated, issues a demand much the way your child requests milk or juice. When their collective thirsts are quenched, you see the way they both thrive in your care. The fussy child becomes satisfied, and the plant reaches toward the sun in a showy display. You might also find that you have to clean the space around your plants much like you would pick up toys and clothes that have been thrown helter-skelter in your toddler's room. Similarly, plants shed spent petals, roses need to be pruned, and weeds need to be pulled. To keep children healthy, parents protect their children against disease with medicine, and gardeners do the same with insect repellent. To nourish them, parents give children vitamins, and gardeners use fertilizer, as both promote healthy growth. As children grow and become adults, they need less and less care. However, here's where the similarity ends. While plants die and become dormant during winter, children still maintain a vital role in the family unit.

Finding the Facts

1. What two things are being compared and contrasted here?

2. In what ways are these two things similar? (There are four similarities; list them here.)

a.

b.

c.

d.

3. In what ways are these two things different? (There is one aspect that is different; write it here.)

Answers

1. The two things being compared and contrasted are a parent and a gardener.

2. Gardeners are like parents in that: a) plants are dependent on gardeners as children are on parents; b) plants require care from gardeners as children do from their parents; c) gardeners tidy up after their plants, as parents do after children; and d) gardeners protect their plants, as parents protect their children.

3. Gardeners are unlike parents in that their responsibility for their plants ends when the plant dies or goes into winter dormancy.

Finding the Main Idea

Now that you've answered those questions, consider one more. Read the previous passage again, and then answer this question:

4. What is the main idea of this passage?

Did you notice that the opening sentence, "Planting a garden is a lot like having a family," is the topic sentence that expresses the main idea of this paragraph? The paragraph does mention a *difference* between these two roles, but notice that the topic sentence does not claim that gardeners and parents are *exactly* alike. Instead, it asserts that they are "a lot" alike.

Transitional Devices

As you read the paragraph about gardeners and parents, did you notice the transitional words and phrases that show you when the writer is comparing (showing similarity) and when the writer is contrasting (showing difference)? Here's the passage once more. As you read it this time, underline the transitional words and phrases you find.

Planting a garden is a lot like having a family. Both require a great deal of work, especially as they grow and as the seasons change. As summer days lengthen, your plants become dependent on you for sustenance, much like your children depend on you for food and drink. Like a thirsty child asking for a drink of water, your plants do the same. Their bent, wilted "body"

language, translated, issues a demand much the way your child requests milk or juice. When their collective thirsts are quenched, you see the way they both thrive in your care. The fussy child becomes satisfied, and the plant reaches toward the sun in a showy display. You might also find that you have to clean the space around your plants much like you would pick up toys and clothes that have been thrown helter-skelter in your toddler's room. Similarly, plants shed spent petals, roses need to be pruned, and weeds need to be pulled. To keep children healthy, parents protect their children against disease with medicine, and gardeners do the same with insect repellent. To nourish them, parents give children vitamins, and gardeners use fertilizer, as both promote healthy growth. As children grow and become adults, they need less and less care. However, here's where the similarity ends. While plants die and become dormant during winter, children still maintain a vital role in the family unit.

There are several transitional words and phrases writers use to show comparison and contrast. In this paragraph, you should have underlined the following words: *much like, in the same way, similarly,* and *however.*

These words and phrases show similarity:

similarly	in the same way
likewise	in a like manner
like	and
just as	also

These words and phrases show difference:

but	yet
on the other hand	on the contrary
however	nevertheless
conversely	

Structure

Now look more closely at the sample paragraph to examine its structure. Exactly how is this paragraph organized?

First, you've noticed that the paragraph begins with a topic sentence that makes the initial comparison: "Gardeners are like parents." Then, the paragraph identifies four ways in which gardeners are like parents:

1. Plants become dependent upon gardeners as children do on parents.

2. Plants require care from their gardeners as children do from parents.

3. Gardeners clean up after their plants as parents do after children.

4. Gardeners protect plants from "dangers" as parents protect children.

Finally, after pointing out these similarities, the paragraph concludes by pointing out an important difference between parents and gardeners:

1. A gardener's responsibility for his or her plants ends with time while a parent's doesn't.

Perhaps you noticed something else in the way this paragraph is organized. Did you notice that every time the paragraph mentions something about a parent's role, it also mentions something about a gardener? Each aspect of the gardener's role is followed by a comparable aspect of the parent's role. Thus, for every aspect of "A" (the gardener), the paragraph provides a comparable aspect of "B" (the parent) to compare or contrast. The paragraph is therefore organized like this: ABABABABAB.

This is called the *point-by-point* method of comparison and contrast. Each aspect of A discussed is immediately paired with that aspect of B (being dependent, requiring care, cleaning up, and protecting).

On the other hand, some writers prefer to deal first with all aspects of A and then with all aspects of B. This is called the *block* method of comparison and contrast; it goes AAAAABBBBB. Here is the same paragraph arranged using the block method:

Planting a garden is a lot like having a family. A plant becomes dependent on the gardener and begs for water on a hot summer day. Gardeners also have to clean up the space around their plants as they shed spent petals, as they require pruning, and as they become choked with weeds. Gardeners also provide for the health of their plants through insecticide and fertilizer applications. A gardener's responsibility for his or her plants lessens as they die at the end of the season or they go into winter dormancy.

Like a gardener, a parent finds their children dependent upon them for food and nourishment. Like a gardener, a parent is constantly picking up after their children, as toys and clothes are scattered throughout the house. Like a gardener, a parent provides for the nourishment and well-being of their children with vitamin supplements, food, and medicines. However, unlike gardeners, parents will find that their responsibility lessens as the child grows, but it does not come to an end.

Here, the passage treats each of the things being compared and contrasted separately—first, all aspects of the gardener, then all aspects of the parent—rather than one aspect of the gardener, one of the parent; another of the gardener, another of the parent. So the organization is quite different.

But you should notice one thing that is similar in both passages: They compare and contrast aspects of A and B that are comparable or parallel. When an aspect of A is discussed, that same aspect of B (whether similar to or different from A) must be discussed. This correspondence of parts is essential for the compare and contrast technique. Look what happens, for example, when the writer does not discuss corresponding parts:

Being a parent is a lot like being a gardener. Parents must bathe, clothe, and feed their children. Parents must also create and maintain guidelines for acceptable behavior for children. Also, parents must see to it that their children get a proper education.

Gardeners nurture the plants in their gardens. They pull weeds and prune them to encourage them to grow. They feed them and apply insecticides. They watch them flower and then witness their demise.

You'll notice that this passage seems to focus on differences between gardeners and parents rather than the similarities. But is this really a fair contrast? Look at the aspects of A (the gardener) that are described here. Do they have any relationship to the aspects of B (the parent) that are described? No. And a compare and contrast passage can't be successful unless the aspects of A and B are discussed comparably. These two paragraphs don't really seem to have a point—there's no basis for comparison between gardeners and parents.

Practice

Suppose you were going to write a paragraph that compares and contrasts readers and detectives. The following are five aspects of being a reader and five aspects of being a detective listed. Only *three* items in each list are comparable. Find those three items in each list and pair them with their matching item. Remember, these items may be either similarities or differences. What's important is that they are comparable aspects.

A reader:

1. Looks for clues to meaning.
2. Has many different types of books to read.
3. Can choose what book to read.
4. Builds vocabulary by reading.
5. Becomes a better reader with each book.

A detective:

1. Has a dangerous job.
2. Gets better at solving crimes with each case.
3. Requires lots of training.
4. Doesn't get to choose which cases to work on.
5. Looks for clues to solve the crime.

Did you find the aspects that are comparable? Did you match reader 1 with detective 5 (similarity)? Reader 3 with detective 4 (difference)? And reader 5 with detective 2 (similarity)? If so, you did terrific work.

Here's how this information might work together in a paragraph:

In many ways, readers are a lot like detectives. Like detectives looking for clues at the scene of the crime, readers look for clues to meaning in the books that they read. And, like detectives who get better and better at solving crimes with each case, readers get better and better at understanding what they read with each book. Unfortunately for detectives, however, they cannot choose which cases they get to work on, whereas readers have the pleasure of choosing which books they'd like to read.

▶ Why Compare and Contrast?

In addition to following the ABABAB or AAABBB structure, compare and contrast passages must, like all other passages, have a point. There's a reason that these two items are being compared and contrasted; there's something the writer is trying to point out by putting these two things side by side for analysis. This reason or point is the main idea, which is often stated in a topic sentence.

The main idea of the first paragraph you looked at in this lesson was, "Planting a garden is a lot like having a family." In this paragraph, you learned that the writer sees a significant similarity between these two roles. Likewise, in the previous paragraph, you see a significant similarity between readers and detectives.

In both cases, you may never have thought of making such comparisons. That's part of the beauty of the compare and contrast organization: It often allows you to see things in a new and interesting way. In addition, it serves the more practical function of showing you how two things measure up against each other so that you can make informed decisions, like about which car to buy (a compare and contrast essay might tell you which car is better) or which savings bond to invest in (a compare and contrast essay will show you which bond is best for you).

Skill Building until Next Time

- As you go through your day, compare and contrast things around you. Compare and contrast, for example, your current job to your previous one. How are they alike? How are they different? Make sure the two things you analyze have comparable aspects. For example, you might want to compare and contrast the salaries, responsibilities, and benefits at both jobs.
- As you make these comparisons, or if you notice compare and contrast passages in what you read, practice arranging them in both point-by-point order (ABABAB) and in block order (AAABBB).

9 ▶ Why Do Things Happen? A Look at Cause and Effect

LESSON SUMMARY

"One thing leads to another"—that's the principle behind cause and effect. Understanding cause and effect, and the relationship between them, will make you a better reader.

For every action," famous scientist Sir Isaac Newton said, "there is an equal and opposite reaction." Every action results in another action (a *reaction*); or, for every action, there is an *effect* caused by that action. Likewise, each action is *caused* by a previous action. In other words, each action has a *cause*—something that made it happen—and each action has an *effect*—something it makes happen.

- **Cause:** a person or thing that makes something happen or produces an effect
- **Effect:** a change produced by an action or cause

Much of what you read is an attempt to explain either the cause of some action or its effect. For example, an author might try to explain the causes of World War I or the effect of underwater nuclear testing; the reason behind a change in policy at work; or the effect a new computer system will have on office procedure. Let's take a look at how writers explaining cause or effect might organize their ideas.

▶ Distinguishing Cause from Effect

A passage that examines cause generally answers the question *why* something took place: Why was the company restructured? Who or what made this take place? A passage that examines effect generally answers the question *what happened* after something took place: What happened as a result of the restructuring? How did it affect the company?

Practice

To help you distinguish between cause and effect, carefully read following the sentences. You'll see that cause and effect work together; you can't have one without the other. That's why it's very important to be able to distinguish between the two. See if you can determine both the cause and the effect in each of the following sentences:

> **Example:** Robin got demoted when she talked back to the boss.
> **Cause:** Robin talked back to the boss.
> **Effect:** Robin got demoted.

1. Inflation has caused us to raise our prices.
   Cause:

   Effect:

2. Since we hired Joan, the office has been running smoothly.
   Cause:

   Effect:

3. He realized that his car had stopped not because it needed repair but because it ran out of gas.
   Cause:

   Effect:

4. The company's budget crisis was created by overspending.
   Cause:

   Effect:

5. As a result of our new marketing program, sales have doubled.
   Cause:

   Effect:

Answers

1. **Cause:** *Inflation*
   Effect: *We had to raise our prices.*
2. **Cause:** *We hired Joan.*
   Effect: *Our office has been running smoothly.*
3. **Cause:** *The car ran out of gas.*
   Effect: *The car stopped.*
4. **Cause:** *Overspending*
   Effect: *Budget crisis*
5. **Cause:** *The new marketing program*
   Effect: *Sales have doubled.*

You were probably guided in your answers to this exercise by the words and phrases that indicate when a cause or effect is being examined. Here is a partial list of such words.

Words Indicating Cause

because (of)	created (by)
since	caused (by)

Words Indicating Effect

since	therefore
hence	consequently
so	as a result

When Cause and Effect Are Interrelated

Notice how the signal words listed on the previous page are used in the following paragraph. Underline the signal words as you come across them.

Ed became a mechanic largely because of his father. His father was always in the garage working on one car or another, so young Ed would spend hours watching his father work. As a result, he became fascinated by cars at an early age. His father encouraged him to learn about cars on his own, so Ed began tinkering with cars himself at age eight. Consequently, by the time he was 13, Ed could tear an engine apart and put it back together by himself. Since he was already so skilled, when he was 15, he got a job as the chief mechanic at a local repair shop. He has been there ever since.

You should have underlined the following signal words and phrases in this paragraph: *because of, so* (twice), *as a result, consequently,* and *since.*

Notice that this paragraph's purpose—to explain *why* Ed became a mechanic—is expressed in the topic sentence, "Ed became a mechanic largely because of his father." This paragraph's purpose, then, is to explain cause, and the primary cause is Ed's father.

You'll notice, however, that some of the sentences in this paragraph also deal with effect. This may seem like a contradiction at first. After all, why would a paragraph about cause deal with effect? But it's not a contradiction. That's because there isn't just *one* thing that led to Ed's becoming a mechanic. Although Ed's dad may have been the initial cause, there was still a *series* of actions and reactions that occurred—a series of causes and effects. Once A causes B, B then becomes the cause for C.

In fact, six different sets of cause and effect are listed in this paragraph. What are they? The first cause is provided to get you started.

Cause 1: Ed's father was always in the garage.

Effect 1:

Cause 2:

Effect 2:

Cause 3:

Effect 3:

Cause 4:

Effect 4:

Cause 5:

Effect 5:

Cause 6:

Effect 6:

Answers

Cause 1: Ed's father was always in the garage.
Effect 1: Ed would spend hours watching.

Cause 2: Ed would spend hours watching.
Effect 2: Ed became fascinated by cars.

Cause 3: Ed became fascinated by cars.
Effect 3: Ed began tinkering with cars.

Cause 4: Ed began tinkering with cars.
Effect 4: Ed's father encouraged him.

Cause 5: Ed's father encouraged him.
Effect 5: Ed could tear an engine apart by himself.

Cause 6: Ed could tear an engine apart by himself.
Effect 6: He got a job as the chief mechanic.

▶ Variations

When One Cause Has Several Effects

Sometimes, one cause may have several effects: Several things may happen as a result of one action. In the following passage, the writer explains several effects of the new marketing campaign:

Our new marketing campaign has been a tremendous success. Since we've been advertising on the radio, sales have increased by 35%. Our client references have doubled, and we've had greater client retention rates. Furthermore, we've been able to hire five new sales representatives and expand our territory to include the southwestern United States.

According to the paragraph, what were the effects of the new marketing campaign?

1.

2.

3.

4.

5.

Answers

1. Sales have increased 35%.
2. Client references have doubled.
3. Client retention rates have increased.
4. Five new sales representatives have been hired.
5. Territory has been expanded to include the Southwest.

When One Effect Has Several Causes

Just as one action can have many results, one action can have many causes as well. The following announcement is an example.

TO: All Commuters
FROM: The Station Management

Unfortunately, we will no longer provide an afternoon snack concession at the train station. Although poor sales are one of the reasons that this service will no longer be provided, there are actually several reasons why the concession is no longer a viable option. In addition to poor sales, the south wall of the train station (where the concession is located) will be undergoing a six-month renovation that will force the closure of the snack concession. In fact, the ticket windows on that wall will be closed as well. Furthermore, from this point forward, the station will close its doors at 6 P.M. due to new town regulations, which will cut the rush-hour commuter traffic coming through the station in half. Finally, Mike

Alberti, the proprietor of the concession has decided to say farewell to his concession business, and after 35 years on the job, Mike will be retiring next month. While none of these factors on their own would have caused the long-term closure of the concession, combined, each makes it impossible to continue running an afternoon snack concession for the foreseeable future.

Why is the afternoon snack concession at the train station being discontinued?

1.

2.

3.

4.

Answers

You should have noticed four causes in the announcement:

 1. Poor sales.
 2. A renovation on the side of the train station where the concession is located.
 3. Town regulations will now close the station at 6 P.M., which will decrease commuter traffic significantly.
 4. The proprietor of the concession has decided to retire.

Contributing vs. Sufficient Cause

You'll notice that the previous announcement informs commuters that "none of these factors on their own would have caused the long-term closure of the concession." This means that each of these causes is a *contributing* cause. A contributing cause *helps* make something happen but can't make that thing happen by itself. It is only one factor that *contributes* to the cause.

On the opposite end of the cause spectrum is the **sufficient** cause. A sufficient cause is strong enough to make something happen by itself. Sufficient cause is demonstrated in the following paragraph.

Dear Mr. Miller:

It has come to our attention that you have breached your lease. When you signed your lease, you agreed that you would leave Apartment 3A at 123 Elm Street in the same state that you found it when you moved in. You also agreed that if the apartment showed signs of damage upon your departure, then we (Livingston Properties) would not return the security deposit that you gave us at the time you moved into the building. Upon inspection, we have found a great deal of damage to the appliances in the apartment as well as the wood floors. Consequently, we will not be returning your security deposit.

Here, you can see that there is one clear reason why Livingston Properties will not return Mr. Miller's security deposit. He breached his lease by damaging the apartment he rented from them. (If you don't know what *breach* means, you should be able to determine the meaning from the context.)

▶ Evaluating Opinions about Cause and Effect

Sometimes, in a cause and effect passage, an author will offer his or her *opinion* about the cause or effect of something rather than *facts* about the cause or effect. In that case, readers must judge the validity of the author's analysis. Are the author's ideas logical? Does he or she support the conclusions he or she comes to? Consider, for example, two authors' opinions about instituting mandatory school uniforms.

Paragraph A

Mandatory school uniforms are a bad decision for our district. If students are required to wear a uniform, it will greatly inhibit their ability to express themselves. This is a problem because dress is one of the major ways that young people express themselves. A school uniform policy also directly violates the freedom of expression that all Americans are supposed to enjoy. Consequently, young people will doubt that their basic rights are protected, and this will affect their larger outlook on civil liberties. Furthermore, school uniforms will interfere with the wearing of certain articles of religious clothing, which will create tensions among certain religious groups that can lead to feelings of discrimination. In addition, school uniforms will place an undue financial burden on many low-income families who may not have the money to spend on new uniforms every year, especially if they have several children. Finally, school uniforms will negate one of the most important concepts we can teach our children—individuality. When push comes to shove, we'd all be better off choosing individuality over uniformity. Mandatory school uniforms are a step in the wrong direction.

Paragraph B

Mandatory school uniforms will have a tremendously positive impact on our district. If students are required to wear a uniform, it will greatly inhibit gang behavior since they will no longer be able to wear gang colors. As a result, schools will experience an overall decrease in school violence and theft. Since violence is one of the major concerns that parents, teachers, and students raise about our district, this change will be welcomed with open arms. In addition, school uniforms will instill a much-needed sense of discipline in our student body, and discipline is something that is, unfortunately, in short supply in our school district. Also, students dressed in uniforms will feel a strong sense of community with their peers, which will lead to a more harmonious school environment. Finally, if students were wearing school uniforms, administrators and teachers would no longer have to be clothing police, freeing them to focus on more important issues than whether someone is wearing a dress that is too short or a T-shirt with an inappropriate message. You can make our schools a better place by supporting mandatory school uniforms.

What effects does the author of paragraph A think mandatory uniforms would have?

1.

2.

3.

4.

5.

What effects does the author of paragraph B think mandatory uniforms would have?

1.

2.

3.

4.

5.

You'll notice that both authors take one cause—mandatory school uniforms—and offer several possible effects. Often, authors will use the cause and effect structure to make arguments like the ones we've just seen: one for and one against mandatory school uniforms. It is up to the reader to determine whose argument seems most valid.

► Summary

Understanding cause and effect is an important skill not only for reading comprehension, but also for your daily life. To analyze the events happening around you, you must be able to understand *why* those events happened—what caused them. Similarly, to make decisions or evaluate the decisions of others, you must be able to consider the effects of a possible decision. "Reading," not only texts but also events and situations, requires you to understand cause and effect.

Skill Building until Next Time

- As you work today, consider the effects of any recent changes in your office, such as new equipment that's been installed, a new system or procedure that's been put in place, a new manager or other employee. How will these changes affect the work place? Your job in particular? Or forecast the effect of changes that are coming. For example, how will the upcoming layoffs affect the company?
- Consider recent events at home or at work. What might have caused them? For example, if a coworker just got a promotion, consider what he or she might have done to get that promotion. Or if a child is having trouble at school, what might be causing that trouble?

10 ▶

Being Structurally Sound: Putting It All Together

LESSON SUMMARY

Today's lesson pulls together what you've learned in Lessons 6–9 and gives you more practice in discerning the structure of a reading passage.

ike an architect designing a building, a writer must have a blueprint—a plan for how he or she will organize the passage. So far in this section, we've looked at several ways that authors may organize their information and ideas:

- **Lesson 6: Chronological order.** Ideas are arranged in the order in which they occurred (or in the order in which they should occur).
- **Lesson 7: Order of importance.** Ideas are arranged in order of *increasing* importance (least important idea to most important idea) or in order of *decreasing* importance (most important idea to least important idea).
- **Lesson 8: Compare and contrast.** Ideas are arranged so that parallel aspects of item A and item B are compared and contrasted either in block style (AAAABBBB) or point-by-point style (ABABABAB).
- **Lesson 9: Cause and effect.** Ideas are arranged so that readers can see what event or series of events *caused* something to take place or what *effect* an event or series of events had.

If any of the terms or strategies on the previous page seem unfamiliar to you, STOP. Please take a few moments to review whatever lesson is unclear.

▶ Practice

Although writers often rely on one particular structure to organize their ideas, in many cases, writers use a combination of these structures. For example, a writer may want to compare and contrast the causes of World War I and those of World War II; or a writer may want to describe, in chronological order, the events that led

to (caused) the failure of the computer system. Thus, today we will look at how writers may combine these strategies. In addition, we'll continue to strengthen your reading comprehension skills by including strategies from the first week:

- Finding the facts
- Determining the main idea
- Defining vocabulary words in context
- Distinguishing between fact and opinion

Practice Passage 1

Begin with the following paragraph. Read it carefully, marking it up as you go. Then answer the questions that follow.

There were several reasons behind our decision to move to Flemington. The first occurred about 18 months ago when Mark and I decided to start a family. We were living in a one-bedroom apartment and we knew that we wanted to move into larger quarters before we had a baby. We began to look at houses. Then, much sooner than expected, I got pregnant. Soon after that, Mark's company announced that they were relocating to Flemington, which was in a less expensive part of the state, about 90 miles south of us. Mark's company had been good to him, and they were one of the few around with excellent benefits, family-friendly policies, and a child-care center on site. With a baby on the way, these things were imperative for us. Since I ran my graphic arts business from home, I wasn't bound to any particular place, so we began looking at real estate in Flemington and also did some research on their school system as well as the overall community. We were very excited about what we found—reasonable housing costs, great schools, and a lively town. Mark then accepted the relocation offer and we found a beautiful old Tudor house. We'll be moving about a month before the baby is due. Let's hope she doesn't decide to come early.

1. Which two organizational strategies does this writer use?
   a. chronological order
   b. order of importance
   c. compare and contrast
   d. cause and effect

2. *Imperative* means
   a. trivial, unimportant.
   b. luxurious, lavish.
   c. pressing, crucial.

3. What prompted the initial decision to move?

4. What happened after the initial cause set things in motion?

a.

b.

c.

d.

e.

f.

Answers

1. a, d. The writer tells you the causes, in the order of which they occurred, that resulted in her move to Flemington.

2. c. The sentence before the one that uses the word *imperative* is describing the attractive family-friendly benefits that Mark's company offers. And since we know that the writer is pregnant, it would make sense that these benefits would be pressing or crucial for her, as opposed to the other two options.

3. The decision to begin a family sparked the initial desire to move.

4. After the writer and her husband decided to start a family, the following events occurred in this order:

a. They began to look at houses.

b. The writer got pregnant.

c. Mark's company announced plan to relocate.

d. The couple began researching real estate, schools, and community life in Flemington.

e. Mark accepted the relocation offer.

f. They found a house.

How did you do? Were you able to see how each cause led to an effect, and how that effect caused something else to happen (another effect)? If you missed any of the questions, here's what you should do:

IF YOU MISSED:	THEN STUDY:
Question 1	Lessons 6 and 9
Question 2	Lesson 3
Question 3	Lesson 9
Question 4	Lesson 9

Practice Passage 2

Now try the passage on the next page. Again, read it carefully, marking it up as you go, and then answer the questions that follow.

There are several changes in the procedure for employees who wish to apply for vacant positions within the company. These changes make it much easier for in-house employees to fill vacancies that occur.

First, the most important difference is that employees will now be notified of all available positions *before* the positions are advertised for the general public. Accordingly, all in-house candidates will be interviewed before we see any outside candidates, and we will offer the job to outside candidates only if no current employees are able to fill the position.

Second, under the new procedure, in-house employees can be hired even if they don't meet all job requirements. Under our old policy, in-house employees had to meet all job qualifications in order to obtain the vacant position. Now, however, employees who have proven themselves dedicated to the company will be hired for a vacant position even if they are lacking some minor qualifications; training will be provided.

A third change involves recommendations. From now on, employees do not need to be recommended for an in-house position before they apply. Instead, employees may apply as soon as they are aware of the vacancy. The remaining procedures and policies (those regarding increase in pay, interview procedure, and hiring approval) remain the same.

5. Which two organizational strategies does this writer use?
  a. chronological order
  b. order of importance
  c. compare and contrast
  d. cause and effect

6. The author organizes his ideas in order of
  a. decreasing importance (most important to least important).
  b. increasing importance (least important to most important).

7. Underline the sentence in this passage that expresses the main idea.

8. The sentence you underlined is a(n)
  a. fact.
  b. opinion.

Answers

5. b, c. The author uses order of importance in comparing the old procedure to the new one.

6. a. The author organizes his ideas in order of decreasing importance. He starts with the most important change ("First, the most important difference is . . .") and moves downward to the second and third most important changes.

7. The sentence that expresses the main idea of all four paragraphs is the second sentence in the first paragraph: "These changes make it much easier for in-house employees to fill vacancies." Although the first sentence tells us what all the paragraphs will be about (the changes in the procedure), it is the second sentence that expresses an opinion— how the author feels about this subject—and therefore, it is the main idea.

8. b. This sentence expresses an opinion, not a fact. There have indeed been changes—that is a fact—but whether those changes make things easier for most employees is debatable. There may be some things about the old procedure that we don't know. Perhaps, for example, they opened the job to both in-house employees and the general public at the same time, but they interviewed all in-house employees first anyway. Because of our limited information about the old procedure, we cannot accept the idea that the change is better as fact.

If you missed some of these questions, now it's up to you to figure out which lessons to review.

Practice Passage 3

Now it's your turn. In this exercise, you'll take a paragraph that is organized one way—by cause and effect—and add another structure: order of importance.

Here's what you should do: Reread the two paragraphs about mandatory school uniforms. Decide which author you agree with most. Then, look carefully at the effects the author predicts. Which effect do you think is most important? Which is least important? Rank these effects in order of importance. Then, decide whether you want to start with the most important idea and end with the least important, or vice versa, start with the least important idea and end with the most important. Finally, put it all together in a paragraph in the space provided.

Paragraph A

Mandatory school uniforms are a bad decision for our district. If students are required to wear a uniform, it will greatly inhibit their ability to express themselves. This is a problem because dress is one of the major ways that young people express themselves. A school uniform policy also directly violates the freedom of expression that all Americans are supposed to enjoy. Consequently, young people will doubt that their basic rights are protected, which will affect their larger outlook on civil liberties. Furthermore, school uniforms will interfere with the wearing of certain articles of religious clothing, and this will create tensions among certain religious groups that can lead to feelings of discrimination. In addition, school uniforms will place an undue financial burden on many low-income families who may not have the money to spend on new uniforms every year, especially if they have several children. Finally, school uniforms will negate one of the most important concepts we can teach our children—individuality. When push comes to shove, we'd all be better off choosing individuality over uniformity. Mandatory school uniforms are a step in the wrong direction.

Paragraph B

Mandatory school uniforms will have a tremendously positive impact on our district. If students are required to wear a uniform, it will greatly inhibit gang behavior since they will no longer be able to wear gang colors. As a result, schools will experience an overall decrease in school violence and theft. Since violence is one of the major concerns that parents, teachers, and students raise about our district, this change will be welcomed with open arms. In addition, school uniforms will instill a much-needed sense of discipline in our student body, and discipline is something that is, unfortunately, in short supply in our school district. Also, students dressed in uniforms will feel a strong sense of community with their peers, which will lead to a more harmonious school environment. Finally, if students were wearing school uniforms, administrators and teachers would no longer have to be clothing police, freeing them to focus on more important issues than whether someone is wearing a dress that is too short or a T-shirt with an inappropriate message. You can make our schools a better place by supporting mandatory school uniforms.

1. Rank the ideas of the paragraph you have chosen in order of their importance to you.

2. Now write a paragraph, choosing whether to put the ideas in the order of increasing importance or decreasing importance.

Skill Building until Next Time

- Look again at the passages you read in Lessons 1–5. What structures do you notice at work in those paragraphs?
- As you read (and write) during the next few days, be aware of the structure of each paragraph you come across. Try to identify the author's strategy; try to use different strategies in your own writing.

Language and Style

In most of the passages you have read so far, the author's ideas and intentions have been very clear. But what happens when they're not? What if the writer doesn't provide a topic sentence that clearly expresses the main idea? Or what if the writer gives you a poem instead of a clear-cut memorandum? How do you figure out what the author is trying to say?

The good news is that no matter how cryptic a piece of writing may seem, the author always leaves clues to help you figure out what he or she means. These clues can be found in the writer's *language* and *style*—the words used and the type of sentences in which he or she uses them. The next four lessons, therefore, focus on four different aspects of language and style:

- Point of view
- Diction
- Style
- Tone

You'll learn how authors use these elements to create meaning for their readers. Then you'll put it all together in Lesson 15 to see how language, style, structure, and meaning work together.

11 ▶ A Matter of Perspective: Point of View

LESSON SUMMARY

This lesson introduces you to the concept of *point of view*, one strategy writers use to convey their meaning to readers. Aspects such as whether writers use the more subjective *I* or the more objective *one*, whether they address readers as *you* or merely refer to an anonymous *they*, influence how readers understand what the writer has written.

Picture this: You are walking along a tree-lined street late in the afternoon. Just ahead of you a woman is sitting on a bench; a dog lies in the shade at her feet. You watch them and nod hello as you walk by.

Now, picture this: You are that dog. You're sitting in the shade under a bench next to your owner's feet. Suddenly, someone walks down the street in front of you. If you look up, you can see that person nod as he or she walks by.

Although you've just pictured the same thing—a person walking by a woman with a dog—you've really pictured two very different scenes, haven't you? The scenario looks quite different from the dog's point of view than from the walker's.

This shift in perspective happens in writing by changing the point of view. *Point of view* is one of the first choices writers make when they begin to write, because it is the point of view that determines who is speaking to the reader.

Point of view is the person or perspective through which the writer channels his or her information and ideas. Just as we may look at a physical object from a number of different perspectives (from above it, below it, behind it, beside it, and so on), we can look at information and ideas from different perspectives as well (mine, yours, his or hers, the professor's, the country's, and so on).

▶ Three Kinds of Point of View

When it comes to expressing point of view, writers can use three distinct approaches:

- **First-person point of view** is a highly individualized, personal point of view in which the writer or narrator speaks about his or her own feelings and experiences directly to the reader using these pronouns: *I, me, mine; we, our, us.*
- **Second-person point of view** is another personal point of view in which the writer speaks directly to the reader, addressing the reader as *you.*
- **Third-person point of view** is an impersonal, objective point of view in which the perspective is that of an outsider (a "third person") who is not directly involved in the action. There is no direct reference to either the reader (second person) or the writer (first person). The writer chooses from these pronouns: *he, him, his; she, her, hers; it, its;* and *they, them, theirs.*

All these points of view are available to writers, but not all of them may be appropriate for what they're writing, and only one will create the exact effect a writer desires. That's because each approach establishes a particular relationship between the reader and the writer.

▶ When Writers Use First Person

Imagine you get one of the following messages from your company's head office:

A. The company congratulates you on the birth of your child.

B. We congratulate you on the birth of your child.

Which message would you rather receive?

Most of us would probably prefer to receive message B over message A. Why? What is the difference between these two messages? Both messages use the second-person point of view, right? They both address the reader as "you." But you probably noticed that the writers chose different points of view to refer to themselves. Message A uses the third-person point of view ("the company") whereas message B uses the first person pronoun "we." As a result, message B seems more sincere because it comes *from* a person *to* a person rather than from "the company" (a thing) to a person (*you*).

But those messages do more than just express congratulations to the reader. They also seem to indicate something about how the people in the head office want to be perceived. In fact, their choice of point of view shows whether they want to be seen as people ("we") or as an entity ("the company"). Read the messages again and then decide how you think each writer wants to be perceived.

Which message seems to tell the reader, "We can speak directly to you because we are real people behind this company"?

Message _____

Which message seems to tell the reader, "We have a very formal relationship; let's not get too personal"?

Message _____

The company that sends message A suggests to the reader that "We have a very formal relationship; let's not get too close or too personal." Message B, on the other hand, tells the reader something more like this: "*We* can speak directly to *you* because we are real people behind this company." Thus, the point of view reflects the way the senders of the message wish to be perceived—as a distant entity (message A) or as friendly colleagues (message B).

Distance vs. Intimacy

Whether writers intend it or not (though they almost always do), the third-person point of view establishes a certain distance between the writer and the reader. There's no direct person-to-person contact that way (*me* to *you*). Rather, with the third-person point of view, someone (or something) else is speaking to the reader.

The first-person point of view, on the other hand, establishes a certain intimacy between the writer and the reader. The writer uses *I, my, mine, we, our,* or *us* as if expressing his or her own personal feelings and ideas directly to the reader. "*We* congratulate you" makes message B much more personal than message A, where *the company* congratulates you.

- First-person point of view establishes intimacy. The writer wants to be close to the reader.
- Third-person point of view establishes distance. The writer wants to distance him- or herself from the reader.

▶ When Writers Use Third Person

In a business environment, it's not always practical to be personal. Though the first-person point of view may make the reader feel close to the writer, the first-person point of view also implies a certain *subjectivity*. That is, the writer is expressing a very personal view from a very personal perspective.

Subjectivity vs. Objectivity

There's nothing wrong with expressing personal views, but in the business world, writers may not always be at an advantage using the first-person point of view. They're more likely to be taken seriously when they're *objective*, presenting things from an outsider's point of view, than when they're *subjective*, presenting things from their own possibly selfish or biased point of view.

- **Subjective:** based on the thoughts, feelings, and experiences of the speaker or writer (first-person point of view)
- **Objective:** unaffected by the thoughts, feelings, and experiences of the speaker or writer (third-person point of view)

Thus, if you wanted to complain about a new office policy, which of the following points of view do you think would be more effective?

A. I think our new office policy is a failure.
B. The new office policy appears to be a failure.

Most people would agree that sentence B is more effective. The question is, *why*?

1. The point of view of sentence B is more effective than that of sentence A because
   a. sentence A is too subjective.
   b. sentence B is too subjective.
   c. sentence A is too objective.
   d. all of the above.

The answer is **a**. Sentence A uses the first-person point of view, and because *I* is so subjective and personal, it doesn't carry as much weight as the objective sentence B. In sentence B, there is no personal perspective; someone from the outside (a third person, not the reader or the writer) is looking at the policy and evaluating it. The third-person point of view is almost always considered to be more objective because the third person is not directly involved in the action. *I*, however, *is* directly involved in the action (the policy) and therefore cannot have an objective opinion about the policy's success or failure. *I*'s opinion may be prejudiced by the writer's personal experience.

Of course, even when a writer uses third person, he or she can still express his or her own opinion. When that opinion is expressed in the third person, however, it *appears* much more objective.

▶ When Writers Use Second Person

When is *you* an appropriate pronoun? What effect does it create for you, the reader? *You* generally is used to address the reader directly, particularly when the writer is giving directions. Imagine, for example, that you have registered for a financial planning class at the local community college. Prior to the first class, you receive the following note:

Note A
As a student in our financial planning class, you will need several items. First, you must purchase the book *Financial Planning: The Basics* by Robin Wexel. Second, you must outline your current financial situation by making a list of your income sources as well as your bank accounts, investments, and retirement plans. Finally, you should prepare a financial wish list that documents where you would like to see yourself financially ten years from now. You should be as specific as possible when putting this list together.

Now, imagine you receive this note instead:

Note B
Students in our financial planning class will need several items. First, they must purchase the book *Financial Planning: The Basics* by Robin Wexel. Second, they must outline their current financial situation by making a list of income sources as well as bank accounts, investments, and retirement plans. Finally, they should prepare a financial wish list that documents where they would like to see themselves financially ten years from now. They should be as specific as possible when putting this list together.

Which note would you rather receive? _____

Most likely you'd rather receive note A. Now, here's the tougher question:

2. The point of view of note A is more effective than the point of view of note B because
   a. note A feels less formal.
   b. note A speaks personally to the reader.
   c. note A addresses the reader as an individual.
   d. all of the above.

Most people would prefer note A for all of these reasons, so the answer is **d**. First of all, in note A, the writer speaks directly to the reader (*you*). In note B, the writer speaks in the third person ("students"); the note never acknowledges that *you* are a student. As a result, note B sounds more formal or official. The second-person point of view, however, addresses you personally. It singles you out as an individual, not as a category (student). It is almost like note A was written just for you.

Second Person and Audience
In fact, because note A uses the second-person point of view, you can make certain assumptions about the audience for this note. Reread note A and then answer this question:

3. Note A was most likely written for
   a. students considering the financial planning class for next year.
   b. instructors at the school.
   c. students enrolled in the financial planning class only.
   d. all students at the community college.

Because note A uses the second-person pronoun *you*, you can assume that it is written for **c**, *only* students enrolled in the financial planning class. It must be, because it can't work for any other audience because of its pronoun.

Note B, on the other hand, could be used for a much larger audience. In fact, the note could be a description in a course catalogue designed for all students at the college as well as the general public. So, the third-person point of view may have been used in note B not to create a distance between the reader and the writer, but to allow for a wider audience.

Writers may also use *you* to make readers feel as if they are taking part in the action or ideas being expressed in the text. For example, let's imagine that a writer wants to convince readers in a particular town that a community garden is a good idea. The writer could use the third-person point of view as in the following paragraph:

Paragraph A

Imagine how wonderful it would be if local residents had access to a community garden. Rather than gardening in isolation, residents would come together in an appealing designated spot to plant a bountiful garden. They would be given a plot of land within the large garden to plant as they see fit. They could plant flowers, vegetables, herbs, or any other greenery they desire. The requirement would be that they spend at least one hour in the garden every week and that they bring a few gardening implements to share, such as watering cans, gardening gloves, fertilizer, and shovels. The benefits of a community garden would be numerous. Residents would have access to land to garden they might not otherwise have. They would be part of a worthwhile and rewarding community activity that would allow them to meet other residents who love gardening and who might have excellent gardening skills and hints to share. Additionally, a community garden would be a wonderful oasis in the middle of our busy town where residents can come to walk, sit, or just enjoy the company of neighbors in a lush and friendly setting.

Or, the writer could use the second-person point of view to express the same ideas:

Paragraph B

Imagine how wonderful it would be if you had access to a community garden. Rather than gardening in isolation, you would come together in an appealing designated spot to plant a bountiful garden. You would be given a plot of land within the large garden to plant as you see fit. You could plant flowers, vegetables, herbs, or any other greenery you desire. The requirement would be that you spend at least one hour in the garden every week and that you bring a few gardening implements to share, such as watering cans, gardening gloves, fertilizer, and shovels. The benefits of a community garden would be numerous. You would have access to land to garden you might not otherwise have. You would be part of a worthwhile and rewarding community activity that would allow you to meet other residents who love gardening and who might have excellent gardening skills and hints to share. Additionally, a community garden would be a wonderful oasis in the middle of our busy town where you can come to walk, sit, or just enjoy the company of neighbors in a lush and friendly setting.

Did you notice the differences between the paragraphs? What pronouns does each paragraph use?

4. Paragraph A uses
   a. first-person pronouns (*I, we*).
   b. second-person pronouns (*you*).
   c. third-person pronouns (*he, she, they*).

5. Paragraph B uses
   a. first-person pronouns (*I, we*).
   b. second-person pronouns (*you*).
   c. third-person pronouns (*he, she, they*).

Paragraph A uses the third person (**c**), while paragraph B uses the second person (**b**). Now, which paragraph do you find more convincing? Most people would be more convinced by paragraph B. Why?

6. Paragraph B seems more convincing because
   a. *you* puts the readers into the action of the paragraph.
   b. *you* makes readers pay more attention.
   c. *you* makes readers imagine themselves in that situation.
   d. all of the above.

The second-person point of view does all of these things (**d**), and that's why it is often more convincing than the other points of view. The second-person point of view puts you, the reader, directly into the situation. As soon as you read that word *you,* you start to pay extra attention because the writer is addressing you directly. And you can't help but imagine yourself enjoy-

ing the benefits of a community garden because the writer puts you in each scenario. The writer of this paragraph knows that if you imagine yourself in these situations, you are much more likely to see the benefits of a community garden.

▶ Summary

You can see by now how important point of view is in writing, for each point of view creates a certain effect. Sometimes, it brings the reader and the writer closer together; sometimes, it pushes them apart. Sometimes, it makes an argument more convincing through third-person objectivity; sometimes, an argument is more convincing through second-person involvement; and sometimes, it's more convincing through first-person intimacy. Writers choose their point of view carefully in order to create a certain relationship both with their ideas and with the reader.

Skill Building until Next Time

- Imagine you have an argument with someone. Tell the story of the argument, first from your point of view using the first-person pronoun. Then, tell the story from the other person's point of view, again using the first-person pronoun. Finally, tell the story from an outsider's point of view using the third-person pronoun. Notice how the story changes when the point of view changes, and notice how both first-person accounts will be subjective, while the third-person account is objective.
- Take a memo or letter you received at work. If the information addresses you in the second person *you,* change it to a third-person point of view (*employees, managers, clients*). Or, if the writer uses the first-person point of view (*I* or *we*), change that to the third-person point of view to eliminate the subjectivity.

12 ▶ Diction: What's in a Word?

LESSON SUMMARY

Today's lesson focuses on *diction*, the words writers choose to convey their meaning. The smallest change in choice of words can significantly change the tone and meaning of a passage. Today's lesson shows you how to pick up on the clues to meaning writers give through their choice of words.

What made Sherlock Holmes such a good detective? Was he just much smarter than everyone else? Did he have some sort of magical powers? Could he somehow see into the future or into the past? No, Sherlock Holmes was no medium or magician. So what was his secret?

His powers of observation.

You may recall that the introduction to this book talked about *active reading*. As an active reader, you should have been marking up the passages you've read in this book: identifying unfamiliar vocabulary, underlining key words and ideas, and recording your reactions and questions in the margin. But there's another part of active reading we haven't talked about: **making observations**.

▶ Making Observations

Making observations means looking carefully at the text and noticing specific things about *how it is written*. You might notice, for example, the point of view the author has chosen. You could also notice:

- Particular words and phrases the writer uses
- The way those words and phrases are arranged in sentences and paragraphs
- Repeated word or sentence patterns
- Important details about people, places, and things

When you make observations, you can then make valid *inferences*. As a matter of fact, you did this in Lesson 11 when you made assumptions about how the writer wanted to be perceived based on the point of view he or she used.

Observations and Inferences

Inferences, as you may recall, are conclusions based on reason, fact, or evidence. Good inferences come from good observations. The observations are the evidence for the inferences. Good inferences—ones based on careful observation—can help you determine meaning, as they helped Sherlock Holmes solve crimes.

To be better readers, then, we need to be more like Sherlock Holmes: We need to be better observers. In the story "The Adventure of the Blanched Soldier," Sherlock Holmes tells a client: "*I see no more than you, but I have trained myself to notice what I see.*" You don't have to be Einstein to be a good reader; you just have to train yourself to notice what you see.

▶ Observing Diction

Test your observation skills on these two sentences:

A. The town's new parking policy, which goes into effect on Monday, should significantly reduce traffic congestion on Main Street.

B. The town's draconian new parking policy, which goes into effect on Monday, should significantly reduce traffic congestion on Main Street.

You don't need Sherlock Holmes's magnifying glass to see the difference between sentence A and sentence B: B uses the words *draconian* and *new* to describe the parking policy, while A uses only *new*. (Go back to Lesson 3 if you've forgotten what *draconian* means.) Now that you have noticed this, why is it important?

1. What does sentence B tell you that sentence A doesn't?
   a. what type of policy is being discussed
   b. how the writer feels about the policy
   c. when the policy begins

The answer is **b**. Both sentences tell you that the policy is a new parking policy, and both say that the policy goes into effect on Monday. But sentence B, because it adds the word *draconian*, tells you how the writer *feels* about the new policy: He doesn't like it. His opinion is implied through his choice of the word *draconian*. Rather than directly saying, "I think the policy is very severe," the writer *suggests* or *implies* that this is the way he feels.

Denotation and Connotation

Now, suppose sentence A also had another adjective to describe the new policy:

A. The town's firm new parking policy, which goes into effect on Monday, should significantly reduce traffic congestion on Main Street.

B. The town's draconian new parking policy, which goes into effect on Monday, should significantly reduce traffic congestion on Main Street.

Do the two sentences now mean the same thing? Yes and no. Both *firm* and *draconian* suggest that the policy is strict, but each word has a specific implication or suggested meaning about *how* strict that policy is. A *firm* policy is not as strict as a *draconian* policy. Furthermore, *draconian* suggests that the policy is not only strict but unfairly or unreasonably so.

So, the words writers choose, even though they may mean the same thing when you look them up in the dictionary, actually have another level of meaning. This is called their connotation. *Connotation* is the implied meaning, the meaning that evolves when the dictionary definition (*denotation*) develops an emotional or social register or a suggestion of degree. The specific words writers choose—their *diction* or word choice—can therefore reveal a great deal about how authors feel about their subjects.

> **Diction:** the particular words chosen and used by the author
> **Denotation:** exact or dictionary meaning
> **Connotation:** implied or suggested meaning

▶ How Diction Influences Meaning

Put your powers of observation to work on the following sentences. Read them carefully and then write down what you notice about each writer's specific choice of words. See if you can use the writers' diction to determine what they are inferring about the seriousness of the situation they are describing:

A. The political parties are meeting with the hopes of clearing up their differences.

B. The political parties have entered into negotiations in an attempt to resolve their conflict.

Both sentences convey the same information: Two parties are meeting because they have a disagreement of some sort to address. But the differences in the diction of each sentence tell us that these two situations aren't exactly the same—or at least that the two writers have different perceptions about the situations. What differences did you notice between these two sentences? List them below (an example has been provided to get you started):

Your Observations:

Example: *I noticed that sentence A says the political parties are "meeting," whereas sentence B says they "have entered into negotiations."*

Now that you've listed your observations, answer this question: In which sentence do you think the situation is more serious, and *why* do you think so? (The *why* is especially important.)

The difference in word choice should tell you that sentence B describes the more serious situation. Here are some of the observations you might have made about the writers' diction that would have told you so:

- The political parties in sentence B are not just "meeting," they've "entered into negotiations." This phrase is often used to describe disagreements between warring parties. And "negotiations" are much more formal than "meetings," suggesting that there is a serious difference to be resolved in sentence B.
- Whereas in sentence A they are ironing things out, the parties in sentence B only "attempt to" resolve the problems. This important difference suggests that the problem between the parties in sentence A is not that serious—the problem is likely to be resolved. In sentence B, on the other hand, "in an attempt" suggests that the problem is quite serious and that it will be difficult to resolve; the outlook is doubtful rather than hopeful.
- In sentence A, the parties are seeking to "clear up their differences," whereas in sentence B, the parties want to "resolve their conflict." The phrase "clear up" suggests that there is merely some sort

of confusion between the two. However, "resolve" suggests that there is a matter that must be solved or settled. And, of course, "conflict" indicates a more serious problem than "differences."

Reading between the Lines

Looking at diction can be especially helpful when the writer's main idea isn't quite clear. For example, in the following paragraph—an excerpt from a letter of recommendation—the author doesn't provide a topic sentence that expresses the main idea. Instead, you must use your powers of observation to answer the question about how the author feels about the described employee.

Paragraph A

Nicole Bryan usually completes her work on time and checks it carefully. She is a competent lab technician and is familiar with several ways to evaluate test results. She has some knowledge of the latest medical research, which has been helpful.

2. What message does the writer of paragraph A convey about Nicole Bryan?
- **a.** Nicole Bryan is an exceptional employee. Hire her immediately!
- **b.** Nicole Bryan is an average employee. She doesn't do outstanding work, but she won't give you any trouble.
- **c.** Nicole Bryan is a lousy worker. Don't even think about hiring her.

To answer this question, you made an inference. Now, support your inference with specific observations about the language in this paragraph. Why do you think your answer is correct? (An example has been provided to get you started.)

Your Observations and Inferences:

Example: *I noticed that the writer says Nicole Bryan "usually" completes her work on time (observation), which suggests that Nicole Bryan is good but not perfect; she doesn't always get her work done on schedule (inference).*

The diction of the paragraph best supports answer **b**: The writer feels that "Nicole Bryan is an average employee. She doesn't do outstanding work, but she won't give you any trouble." You might have supported this inference with observations like these:

- The writer uses the word *usually* in the first sentence, which means that Nicole Bryan is good, but not great; she doesn't always meet deadlines.
- The writer describes Nicole Bryan as a "competent" lab technician. This tells us that Nicole Bryan does her work well enough for the position, but she is not exceptional. She could be better.
- The writer tells us that Nicole Bryan is "familiar with" several ways to evaluate test results. This means that she can do her work using those evaluation techniques, but she is no expert and does not know all there is to know about evaluating test results.
- The writer tells us that Nicole Bryan has "some knowledge of the latest medical research," which tells us that Nicole Bryan knows a little, but not a lot; again, she's better than someone who knows nothing, but she's no expert.

Now, take a look at a revised letter of recommendation. The diction (the word choice) has been changed so that the paragraph sends a different message. Read the paragraph carefully and determine how the writer feels about Nicole Bryan:

Paragraph B

Nicole Bryan always submits her work promptly and checks it judiciously. She is an excellent lab technician and has mastered several ways to evaluate test results. She has an extensive knowledge of the latest medical research, which has been invaluable.

3. What message does the writer of paragraph B convey about Nicole Bryan?
   a. Nicole Bryan is an exceptional employee. Hire her immediately!
   b. Nicole Bryan is an average employee. She doesn't do outstanding work, but she won't give you any trouble.
   c. Nicole Bryan is a lousy worker. Don't even think about hiring her.

This time you should have chosen answer **a**. The change in diction tells you that this writer thinks Nicole Bryan is a fantastic employee. To ensure the difference in word choice is clear, write the words used in paragraph B to replace the words in paragraph A. The first replacement has been filled in to get you started.

PARAGRAPH A	PARAGRAPH B
usually	always
on time	
carefully	
competent	
is familiar with	
some knowledge	
helpful	

▶ Summary

Just as Sherlock Holmes learned to notice what he saw when he arrived at the scene of a crime, you can also learn to notice what you see when you look carefully at a piece of writing. By noticing the specific words a writer has chosen to use, you can help ensure that you fully comprehend the writer's message.

Skill Building until Next Time

- Think about how you choose the words you use when you speak to people. Do you use different types of words for different people? Do you think carefully about what you say and which words you will use? How much are you aware of your own diction?

- Notice how much the meaning of a sentence can change when a single word is altered. Form a simple sentence, like: "Experts say the economy is *unhealthy*." Now, replace "unhealthy" with synonyms that have slightly different connotations, like: *sick, feeble, ill, dying, under the weather, feverish, infected*. Each word will express a slightly different attitude about your subject to the reader. Insert each of these words into your sentence and see how much the meaning is altered. (This exercise will work well if you choose words, like *rich*, *tired*, *happy*, or *sad*, that have many synonyms with a wide range of connotations.)

13 ▶ Style: It's Not What They Say but How They Say It

LESSON SUMMARY

How a writer puts words together to express meaning is as important as *what* the writer says. This lesson shows you how to analyze the style of a piece of writing in order to get a better understanding of what the writer means.

Style?" you ask. "What does style have to do with reading comprehension?"

Actually, style has a good deal to do with reading comprehension. Just as writers use different structures to organize their ideas and information, they also use different styles to express their ideas and information. Thus, the more aware you are of the elements of style, the more successfully you can determine a writer's purpose and understand his or her ideas.

Style is also important because it is often what attracts us to, or repels us from, certain writers or types of writing. Though an awareness of style might not make us change our taste, it can at least help us appreciate different writers and different styles.

Style: a distinctive way of writing or speaking or doing something; the manner in which something is done

▶ What Is Style?

Style, in writing, generally consists of three elements:

1. Sentence structure
2. Degree of detail and description
3. Degree of formality

Diction is also an aspect of style, but because diction is so essential to meaning, it had its own lesson in this book.

Sentence Structure

Looking at sentence structure means looking at the type of sentences the writer has used. Are they short, simple sentences? Or are they long and complex, with a lot of clauses and phrases? Or does the writer use a mix? Does every sentence sound the same, or is there variety in the word order and structure? Is the complexity or simplicity of the sentences at the right level for the readers?

Read the following sentences and then answer the questions that describe their sentence structure.

A. The meeting began. Mr. Thomas described the policy. Then, Mr. Underwood spoke in favor of it. Afterward, Ms. Villegas spoke against it.
B. After the meeting, when everyone had already left the room, Ms. Villegas stayed behind to speak with Mr. Thomas. She carefully explained her position on the new policy, hoping she'd get him to change his mind.

1. Which version uses simple sentences?
   a. version A
   b. version B

2. Which version uses the same sentence structure throughout?
   a. version A
   b. version B

3. Which version uses complex sentences?
   a. version A
   b. version B

4. Which version varies the sentence structures, using different kinds of sentences?
   a. version A
   b. version B

You probably noticed that version A is the one that uses simple sentences with essentially the same sentence structure throughout. (You might also have noticed that these sentences sound rather dull because they are so simple and unvaried.) In version B, the sentences are far more complex with more variation in their structure.

Degree of Detail and Description

When you look at degree of detail and description, ask two things:

1. How specific is the author? Does he write "dog" (general) or "Labrador retriever" (specific detail)? Does she write "some" (general) or "three and a half pounds" (specific detail)?
2. How much description does the author provide? Does he write "Mr. B is my manager" (non-descriptive) or "Mr. B, my manager, is a tall man with piercing eyes and a mustache" (descriptive)? Or, does he go even further: "Mr. B, my manager, is six foot ten with eyes that pierce like knives and a mustache like Hitler's" (very descriptive)?

Try your hand at deciding whether words are specific and descriptive or general and nondescriptive.

5. Which of the following word(s) or phrases are more specific and descriptive? Underline them. Which words or phrases are more general and nondescriptive? Circle them.

a. car

b. red 1968 Ford

c. on the corner of 58th and Broadway

d. on the corner

As you could probably tell, answers **b** and **c** are the more specific and descriptive ones, while answers **a** and **d** are more general and nondescriptive.

Degree of Formality

The *degree of formality* of a piece of writing has to do with how formal or casual the writer's language is. For example, does the writer use slang as if speaking to a friend, or jargon (specific, technical language) as if speaking to colleagues? Does the writer address the reader by his or her first name (casual), or by his or her title (formal)?

6. Which sentences are more informal? Underline them. Which are more formal? Circle them.

a. Let's get together after work on Thursday.

b. We kindly request that you join us for a social gathering at the close of business on Thursday.

c. These figures indicate the sales have increased significantly.

d. Sales are up!

Chances are that you didn't have much trouble deciding that sentences **a** and **d** are more informal and sentences **b** and **c** are more formal.

▶ How the Three Elements of Style Work Together

Look at how these three elements of style work together in the following two letters. Both convey essentially the same information, but they are written in radically different styles. Read the letters carefully and then list your observations. What do you notice that's different between these two letters?

Letter A

Lucy:

Listen, a while ago, I ordered some invitations from your website. I haven't gotten them yet. What happened? Where are they? Find out! I need them!

—Isabel

Letter B

Dear Ms. Mirabella:

Three weeks ago, on April 14, I rush ordered two boxes of personalized party invitations from your website (Order #123456). To date, I have not received my order. Please look into this matter immediately as I am in dire need of this product.

Sincerely,

Ms. Lindsey

What did you notice about these two letters? How are they different? Consider sentence structure, degree of description and detail, and degree of formality. List your observations in the space below (an example has been provided to get you started):

Your Observations:

Example: *I notice that letter A addresses the reader as "Lucy," whereas letter B addresses her as "Ms. Mirabella."*

Now, answer the following questions:

7. Which letter is more formal?
  a. letter A
  b. letter B

8. Which letter seems to have been written by someone who knows the recipient well?
  a. letter A
  b. letter B

9. In which letter is the sentence structure more complex?
  a. letter A
  b. letter B

10. Which letter is more descriptive and detailed?
  a. letter A
  b. letter B

You probably noticed immediately the difference in degree of formality between these two letters. Letter A is written in a very casual style, as if the writer knows the reader very well and therefore does not need to use a professional approach. Our first clue to this casual relationship is the way the letter is addressed. Letter A addresses the reader as "Lucy," while letter B begins with a formal "Dear Ms. Mirabella." The same difference can be seen in the closing of the letters: "Isabel" vs. "Sincerely, Ms. Lindsey."

The (in)formality of each relationship is also reflected in the sentence structure and degree of description and detail. You probably noticed, for example, that letter A uses short, choppy sentences, and exclamation points, which make the letter sound less formal, more urgent, and more demanding. The writer also uses casual words like "listen" so that the writing sounds conversational. On the other hand, letter B uses longer, more complex sentences to make the letter sound more formal and sophisticated.

At the same time, you probably noticed that letter A does not provide the kind of specific information that letter B does. Letter A tells us the writer placed an order for "some invitations" "a while ago," but letter B tells us the order was placed "three weeks ago, on April 14" and that the order was for "two boxes of personalized party invitations." The fact that letter A does not provide specific details is further evidence that the reader knows the writer very well, for the writer doesn't have to provide specific details. Furthermore, in letter A, the writer uses a command—"Find out!"—whereas in letter B, the writer *asks,* rather than demands, that the matter be looked into. This politeness reflects a professional distance between writer and reader.

In business, as in most writing, the audience usually determines the writer's style. The writer of letter A is probably capable of writing in the style of letter B, but because she has a casual relationship with her reader, she doesn't need to use a formal style.

The Effect of Description and Detail

In business, what some people call "flowery" style—lots of description and detail—is almost never appropriate. Why? Because in business, as they say, "time is money," so readers don't want to spend time reading lengthy descriptions or extensive detail. They just want the facts: when the meeting will be held and where; what the new product is designed to do and how much it costs; how the new training manual is coming along. In most cases, the more straightforward, the better.

Other times, however, when they want readers to imagine a situation or to experience something through language, writers need a "flowery" style. That is, they need a high degree of description and detail. The following two paragraphs show the difference. Both describe the same appointment, but in two very different styles. One is written in a style appropriate to business and only records the facts. The other describes the meeting in a style appropriate for general readers interested in the feelings of the people involved.

Paragraph A

Yesterday at 10:00 A.M., Mark Spencer held a press conference. Eleanor Cartwright was present as well. Mr. Spencer talked about upcoming events at the Smithfield Museum of Art, where he is Director. Then he announced that Eleanor Cartwright had just been appointed Director of Development. This new position was created due to the planned building of a new wing, which will house the significant art collection that was donated to The Smithfield Museum last year. Mr. Spencer outlined Ms. Cartwright's qualifications and introduced her to the press. She discussed plans for the new wing, and she also took several questions from reporters before the press conference ended.

Paragraph B

Yesterday at 10:00 A.M., Mark Spencer, the popular Director of the Smithfield Museum of Art, held a press conference. The room was buzzing with reporters as Mr. Spencer took the podium. Standing to his right was a striking woman with a crimson suit. Mr. Spencer first discussed the soon-to-be-launched artist-in-residence program as well as the upcoming annual fundraising dinner, which has been the hottest ticket in town ever since Mr. Spencer came to the Smithfield.

The room was thick with curiosity as Mr. Spencer turned toward the mysterious woman and invited her to join him at the podium. Mr. Spencer then spoke in an excited and genuine tone, "I'm delighted to introduce to you, the new Director of Development of the Smithfield Museum, Ms. Eleanor Cartwright." Mr. Spencer explained that this position was created due to the building of the new wing, for which construction is scheduled to start soon. The wing will house the impressive and significant art collection of Mr. and Mrs. Martin Buckner, which was donated to the museum last year. Mr. Spencer listed Ms. Cartwright's impressive

credentials as the reporters hung on every word. Finally, Ms. Cartwright took the podium and wowed everyone with details about the new wing. She also took several questions. By the time she was done, everyone in attendance was charmed by her wit and sophistication and they left the room convinced that the Smithfield Museum, once barely known, was truly becoming a major force in the art world.

Now, write down your observations about these two paragraphs below. How are these two versions different? What did you notice about the sentence structure? About the degree of description and detail? About the degree of formality?

Your Observations:

Example: *I noticed that version B is almost twice as long as version A.*

Now, use your observations to answer the following questions:

11. Which version tells you more about Mark Spencer?
a. paragraph A
b. paragraph B

12. Which version tells you more about Eleanor Cartwright?
a. paragraph A
b. paragraph B

13. Which version is more objective?
   a. paragraph A
   b. paragraph B

14. Which version makes you feel excited about Eleanor Cartwright's appointment?
   a. paragraph A
   b. paragraph B

You noticed, of course, that paragraph B is much more descriptive than paragraph A—it tells you more about both Mark Spencer and Eleanor Cartwright. Paragraph A just provides the facts—specific details, but no description. Paragraph A is very objective. We do not learn anything about Mark Spencer other than his job title. For example, we don't know how people feel about him. In paragraph A, we also learn very little about Eleanor Cartwright other than her new job. We don't know what she looks like or how people in the room respond to her.

Paragraph B, however, tells us about Mark Spencer's reputation ("popular" and responsible for making the annual fundraising dinner "the hottest ticket in town"). Paragraph B also provides many details about Eleanor Cartwright ("striking woman with a crimson suit," "impressive credentials"). We also learn a good deal about the general tone of the room and how this announcement was received ("the room was buzzing," "reporters hung on her every word," "they left the room convinced that the Smithfield Museum, once barely known, was truly becoming a major force in the art world"). All these details help us feel something about the announcement and the people involved because the characters and the situation are presented visually; we can almost see what happens.

▶ Summary

Style, as you can see, is an important aspect of reading comprehension. It can tell us about the writer's relationship to the reader; it can distance us with its objectivity or draw us in with its description and detail. As readers, we tend to react strongly to style, often without knowing why. But now you do know why, and you can use that knowledge to help you understand what you read.

Skill Building until Next Time

- As you come across sentences or paragraphs written in different styles, see how they would sound if the style were altered. Change the level of formality, the degree of description and detail, or the sentence structure to create a new style.
- Do you have a favorite author? Take a second look at a particularly memorable work by this author, paying close attention to the style elements at work. If you are a Jane Austen fan, pick out features that make her novels enjoyable for you. Do you like her degree of formality, the way she uses detail to describe fancy parties, or the way she varies her sentence structure? After you've taken a close look at this work, try your own hand at it. Can you write a letter to a friend in the same style that Jane Austen would have? How about Ernest Hemingway or Stephen King?

14 ▶ How They Say It, Part Two: Tone

LESSON SUMMARY

The way you perceive a person's tone of voice has a great deal to do with how you understand what that person is saying. The same is true of tone in writing; it's vital to pick up on clues to tone in order to understand a written piece fully. This lesson shows you how.

Say this word out loud: "Sure."

How did you say it? Did you say it with a smile, as in "Sure, anytime"? Or did you say it flatly, as if responding to a command? Or did you stretch the word out, "*Suuuurre*," as if you didn't believe what someone just said? Or did you ask it, as in, "Are you *sure* this is okay?"

Perhaps you didn't realize there were so many ways to say this one single word, "sure." But there are. Why? The word itself isn't different; its denotation (dictionary meaning) isn't different; so how can the same word express so many different things?

The difference in the meaning of all these *sure*s comes from the tone—how you say the word, and thus how your listeners will feel when they hear you say it.

Tone: the mood or attitude conveyed by words or speech

When you speak and listen, you can hear the tone of your voice as well as the tone of the person to whom you are speaking. But how do you catch tone in writing? How do you know how the writer wants his or her words to sound? "Sure" by itself doesn't tell us whether you should whisper or shout it. You need to look at the context surrounding that word to find clues about the proper tone to use.

Think about how tone is created in speech. When you say "sure," the tone changes according to how loudly or softly you say the word and how slowly or quickly you say it. Tone is also conveyed (or supported) by the speaker's expressions and body language. In writing, of course, you do not have these visual resources, but you do have plenty of clues to help you determine tone. Those clues come from the elements of language and style that you've studied so far: point of view, diction, and style.

▶ How Tone Influences Meaning

It may help you to think of a sentence as a collection of ingredients (words and phrases) that result in a dish (idea). These elements of language and style are like the spices that you need to give that sentence a certain flavor. Different spices will result in a different flavor (tone).

Look at the following two letters. Both convey essentially the same information, but they have two rather different tones.

Letter A
Dear Client:

Thank you for your letter. We will take your suggestion into consideration. We appreciate your concern.

Letter B
Dear Valued Customer:

Thank you for your recent letter regarding our refund policy and procedure. We are taking your suggestion quite seriously and truly appreciate your concern.

Which of these letters has a more positive tone? As you can see, letter B is more positive. Why? What do you notice about letter B that is different from letter A? List your observations below:

Example: *I noticed that letter A is addressed "Dear Client," while letter B is addressed "Dear Valued Customer."*

Perhaps you noticed that letter B uses key words like "*valued* customer" and "*truly* appreciate." Letter B also refers to the specific contents of the reader's letter, thus letting the reader know that his or her letter has been read. Furthermore, letter B tells the reader not just that the company "will take your suggestion into consideration"—which sounds a bit like an empty promise—but that the writers are taking the suggestion "quite seriously."

You may also notice that the sentences in letter B are longer than those in letter A, whose sentences are shorter and somewhat choppy. If you read those short sentences out loud, how do they sound? They're not very inviting, are they? They sound somewhat mechanical and empty of any feeling.

Use your observations to answer the following questions.

1. The tone of letter A is best classified as
 a. sincere.
 b. complimentary.
 c. indifferent.

Choice **c**, indifferent, best describes the tone of letter A. There is no indication that the writers of letter A have actually read their client's letter, so there's no indication that they plan to take the client's suggestion seriously. They are indifferent to it. Also, the sentence structure indicates that the writers have not put much thought into writing this letter; as a result, the sentences sound abrupt and even unappreciative.

2. The tone of letter B is best classified as
 a. cheerful.
 b. sincere.
 c. apologetic.

In contrast to letter A, the writers of letter B are **b**, sincere. They know exactly what their customer wrote about—there's the importance of specific details again! They've also taken the time to individualize the letter; and they've added words that show they value their customer and their customer's feedback.

Varieties of Tone

Just as there are endless varieties of tone when we speak, there are endless varieties of tone in writing.

Here's a short list of some of the more common words used to describe a writer's tone:

cheerful	sarcastic
complimentary	ironic
hopeful	wistful
sad	foreboding
gloomy	playful
apologetic	sincere
critical	insincere
insecure	authoritative
disrespectful	threatening
humorous	indifferent

If any of these terms are unfamiliar to you, please look them up in a dictionary now.

Practice

Now look at several sentences and paragraphs to see if you can correctly identify their tone. As you read them, think of how the paragraphs sound. You may even want to read them out loud. With what kind of voice do you read? What's your tone? Use your instincts, as well as your observations, to choose the correct tone for each paragraph. Answers and explanations come immediately after the practice paragraphs.

3. I think the theme of this novel probably has something to do with revenge.
 a. playful
 b. uncertain
 c. cheerful

4. Without a doubt, the theme of this novel is revenge.
 a. gloomy
 b. disrespectful
 c. authoritative

5. Your essay? Oh, it was just fabulous. Really, I've never seen anything like it.
   a. insincere
   b. critical
   c. disrespectful

6. This is one of the best essays I've ever seen. It's clear, concise, and convincing.
   a. complimentary
   b. wistful
   c. hopeful

7. Bill had stayed up all night preparing for this presentation. He had everything ready: charts, graphs, lists, statistics. This was the biggest meeting of his career. He was ready. He smiled as the cab pulled up to 505 Park Avenue, and he gave the taxi driver an extra large tip. He entered the building confidently and pushed #11 on the elevator. Suddenly, as the doors of the elevator closed, he realized that he had left his briefcase in the cab.
   a. cheerful
   b. ironic
   c. critical

Answers

3. b. The writer is obviously afraid to be authoritative and uses phrases like "I think," "probably," and "something to do with" to reflect this uncertainty.

4. c. The writer is clearly comfortable in making a definitive statement. There is no hesitation in the tone here. Instead of suggesting, the writer declares: "Without a doubt…"

5. a. Because of the opening question and because the next sentences are so vague, a reader can assume that the writer either hasn't read the essay or didn't like it. Also, "really" indicates that the writer is afraid the reader won't be convinced by the statement, so he tries to emphasize it. Furthermore, "I've never seen anything like it" isn't necessarily a compliment—it could really mean many different things, not all of them good.

6. a. Unlike question 5, this paragraph really is complimentary. The writer specifies three things that make the reader's essay exceptional: It's "clear, concise and convincing." The use of more specific adjectives makes this writer's praise seem sincere.

7. b. *Irony* is the mood created when things happen in a manner that is opposite of what was expected to happen. Here, Bill had prepared diligently for the big meeting and had everything ready. But contrary to his expectations of having a very successful presentation, he had no presentation at all because he left his materials in the taxi cab. The irony is heightened by his confidence.

▶ Summary

An ability to determine tone is an essential component of reading comprehension. Often, writers will let their tone convey their meaning, so you need to look carefully for clues in the writer's language and style to determine how writers want their words to sound.

Skill Building until Next Time

- Listen carefully to people today and notice how much you depend on tone to determine exactly what people mean when they speak to you. Notice also how you use tone to convey meaning when you speak to other people.
- Go back to the practice exercise where you identified the tone of those five passages. Try changing the tone of some of those passages.

15 ▶ Word Power: Putting It All Together

LESSON SUMMARY

This lesson pulls together what you've learned in Lessons 11–14, as well as in previous lessons. It shows you how to use point of view, diction, style, and tone to understand what a writer means.

You've learned a lot this week about language and how much it affects meaning. Before you add this knowledge to the knowledge you already have about structure and the basics of reading comprehension, take a minute for a brief review of the last four lessons. It's always a good idea to stop and review material you've learned before you go on to new material.

▶ Review: Language and Style

Point of view is the perspective from which the writer speaks. Sometimes, writers use the first-person point of view (*I, me, my, we, our, us*) to express their personal feelings and experiences directly to the reader. This point of view creates a sense of intimacy between the reader and the writer because it expresses an extremely subjective perspective. When writers use the second-person point of view, they address the reader directly by using the pronoun *you*. This point of view is often used to give directions and to make the reader feel directly involved in the action described by the writer. The third-person point of view is the objective perspective of a "third person," someone who is not directly involved in the action or ideas expressed in the passage. This point of view establishes a distance between the reader and writer and uses the pronouns *he, his, him; she, hers, her; it, its;* and *they, them,* and *their.*

Diction refers to the specific words chosen by the author to express his or her ideas. Because words have both a *denotation* (exact or dictionary meaning) and a *connotation* (implied or suggested meaning), as well as an emotional register, the words an author chooses are very significant. Authors, like politicians, must choose their words carefully to express exactly the right idea with exactly the right impact.

Style is the manner in which the writers express their ideas in writing. Style is composed of three main elements: sentence structure, degree of description and detail, and degree of formality. Some writers use a very formal style; others may write in a casual style. Certain styles are best for particular audiences or purposes. For example, a high degree of formality with specific details but without any unneccessary description would be appropriate for business, where time is money and writers should get to the point as quickly as possible.

Finally, *tone* is the mood or attitude conveyed by the writing. Tone is created by a combination of point of view, diction, and style. Tone is extremely important in determining meaning because as we noted, a word as simple as "sure" can have many different meanings depending upon the tone in which it is said. To determine the tone, you have to look for clues as to how the writer wants his or her words to sound.

> **If any of these terms or ideas sound unfamiliar to you, STOP. Please take a few minutes to review whatever lesson is unclear.**

▶ Practice

In today's practice, you'll combine these aspects of language with everything else you've learned in this book about reading comprehension:

- Finding the facts
- Determining the main idea
- Determining vocabulary meaning through context
- Distinguishing facts and opinions
- Chronological order
- Cause and effect
- Compare and contrast
- Order of importance

Practice Passage 1

Begin with a paragraph someone might see in a local newspaper: a profile of a town figure. Read the paragraph carefully, marking it up as you go, and write your observations in the space provided.

Ms. Crawford has been a model citizen since she moved to Springfield in 1985. She started out as a small business owner and quickly grew her business until it was one of the major employers in the region. In 1991, her company was profiled in *Business Week* magazine. Her innovative business model includes a great deal of community work and fundraising, the rewards of which have brought deep and lasting benefits to Springfield and its citizens. Today, she is being honored with Springfield's Citizen of the Century Award to honor all her cutting-edge efforts on behalf of our community.

Your Observations:

Now answer the following questions:

1. Ms. Crawford's company was profiled in *Business Week*
   a. in 1985.
   b. in 1991.
   c. today.

2. Which sentence best sums up the main idea of the paragraph?
   a. Ms. Crawford is very smart.
   b. Ms. Crawford is a dedicated citizen.
   c. Springfield would be nowhere without Ms. Crawford.

3. "Ms. Crawford has been a model citizen since she moved to Springfield in 1985" is
   a. fact.
   b. opinion.
   c. point of view.

4. "Innovative" means
   a. helpful.
   b. remarkable.
   c. inventive.

5. This paragraph is organized according to what structure?
   a. cause and effect
   b. compare and contrast
   c. chronological order
   d. order of importance

6. This paragraph uses what point of view?
   a. first-person point of view
   b. second-person point of view
   c. third-person point of view

Answers

1. a. "In 1991, her company was profiled in *Business Week* magazine."

2. b. While it does seem that Ms. Crawford must be very smart since she has been so successful, that is not the main idea that governs the whole paragraph. Instead, the paragraph highlights her dedication to the town and local community since she moved there. Answer **c** can't be correct because although the paragraph indicates that Ms. Crawford is very valuable, it does not say that Springfield would be nowhere without her. This is an inference you might make but cannot support.

3. b. Although the sentence does contain fact (Ms. Crawford moved to Springfield in 1985), the sentence makes an assertion about those years since 1985: Ms. Crawford has been a model citizen all those years. This is an assertion, an opinion that needs evidence. The rest of the paragraph provides that evidence.

4. c. The best clue to determine the meaning of this word is found in the last sentence, which says that Ms. Crawford is being honored for "all her cutting-edge efforts on behalf of our community." Since her efforts on behalf of the community have been "cutting-edge," we can assume that her business model, which includes a great deal of community work and fundraising and is described as *innovative,* must also be *cutting-edge.* Therefore, the definition of *innovative* must be similar to *cutting-edge,* so the likely choice is *inventive.*

5. c. The paragraph follows Ms. Crawford's contribution to the community from the time she moved to Springfield in 1985 to the present.

6. c. This paragraph uses the objective third-person point of view. There is no *I* or *we* (first person) or *you* (second person), and the only pronouns the paragraph uses are the third-person pronouns *she* and *her*.

How did you do? If you got all six answers correct, good work. This table shows you which lesson to study for each question you missed.

IF YOU MISSED:	THEN STUDY:
Question 1	Lesson 1
Question 2	Lesson 2
Question 3	Lesson 4
Question 4	Lesson 3
Question 5	Lesson 6
Question 6	Lesson 11

Practice Passage 2

Now try another paragraph. Don't forget to mark it up as you read and make observations. Pay special attention to language and style.

There will be dire consequences for residents if a shopping mall is built on the east side of town. First, the shopping mall will interfere with the tranquil and quiet atmosphere that we now enjoy. Second, the mall will attract a huge number of shoppers from a variety of surrounding areas, which will result in major traffic congestion for those of us who live here. But most importantly, to build the shopping mall, many of us will be asked to sell our homes and relocate, and this kind of displacement should be avoided at all costs.

7. The main idea of this passage is that the shopping mall would
   a. be great for the community.
   b. not change things much.
   c. be bad for the community.

8. "Tranquil" means
   a. calm.
   b. disturbing.
   c. chaotic.

9. This passage is organized
   a. in chronological order.
   b. by cause and effect.
   c. by order of importance.
   d. both **a** and **c**.
   e. both **b** and **c**.

10. This passage uses which point of view?
   a. first person
   b. second person
   c. third person

11. This passage is written from whose perspective?
   a. that of the residents
   b. that of an outside consultant
   c. that of the shopping mall developer

12. The choice of the word "dire" suggests that the consequences of the merger would be
   a. minimal.
   b. expected.
   c. disastrous.

13. Which words best describe the style of this passage?
   a. informal, conversational
   b. descriptive, story-like
   c. formal, business-like

14. The tone of this passage is
   a. sad.
   b. foreboding.
   c. threatening.

Answers

7. c. The first sentence is the topic sentence, which establishes that the shopping mall will be bad for residents of the town. The remaining sentences support that idea.

8. a. This paragraph tells us how the shopping mall will change the town. The sentence with the word "tranquil" calls the town tranquil and quiet, and it says that the mall will interfere with these qualities. Since a mall by nature is big and busy, it is likely that it will interfere with opposite kinds of qualities. Since "tranquil" and "quiet" are used together, it is likely that they are similar in nature. Therefore, "tranquil" obviously means calm, not disturbing or chaotic.

9. e. The writer warns the readers of the effects that a shopping mall will have on residents of the town and arranges those effects in order of importance, saving the most important effect for last.

10. a. The first-person point of view is reflected in the use of the pronouns *us* and *we*.

11. a. The writer says that the shopping mall will have "dire consequences" for the residents and then uses the pronouns *us* and *we*—which identifies the writer with the residents—when listing those dire consequences.

12. c. The effects the writer includes here are all very serious, especially the third effect—displacement. The writer has chosen the word "dire" to emphasize that seriousness.

13. c. The passage avoids any unnecessary description or details and uses formal rather than casual language.

14. b. Each sentence explains a negative effect that the shopping mall will have on the residents and the negativity of this passage is heightened by the word "dire" and the phrase "avoided at all costs." Though the shopping mall itself might be described as threatening, (choice **c**), the writer is not "threatening" anybody.

How did you do? Once again, congratulations if you got them all correct. If not, this table tells you what to do.

IF YOU MISSED:	THEN STUDY:
Question 7	Lesson 2
Question 8	Lesson 3
Question 9	Lessons 7 and 9
Question 10	Lesson 11
Question 11	Lesson 11
Question 12	Lesson 12
Question 13	Lesson 13
Question 14	Lesson 14

Skill Building until Next Time

- Review the Skill Building sections from Lessons 6–14. Try any Skill Builders you didn't do.
- Write a paragraph about what you've learned in the last two weeks about structure and language. Begin your paragraph with a clear topic sentence, such as "I've learned a lot about how writers use structure and language." Then, write several sentences that support or explain your assertion. Try to use at least one new vocabulary word in your paragraph.

Reading between the Lines

Now that you've studied the way authors use structure and language to organize and express their ideas, you're ready to tackle more difficult passages: those in which the writers don't provide clear topic sentences or do not clearly indicate their intentions. To understand this type of text, you have to "read between the lines." This means you have to really put your observation skills to use and scour the passage for clues to meaning. Like Sherlock Holmes, you will really have to notice what you see.

By the end of this section, you should be able to:

- Determine an implied main idea
- Determine an implied cause or effect
- Distinguish between logical and emotional appeals
- Determine the theme of a piece of literature

You'll look at a variety of texts, including some literature, and then put it all together in a review lesson.

16 ▶ Finding the Implied Main Idea

LESSON SUMMARY

This lesson shows you how to determine the main idea of a passage in which the writer has not provided a topic sentence or otherwise spelled it out for you.

O h, the power of suggestion. Advertisers know it well—and so do writers. They know that they can get an idea across to their readers without directly saying it. Instead of providing a topic sentence that expresses their main idea, many times, they simply omit that sentence and instead provide a series of clues through structure and language to get their ideas across.

Finding an implied main idea is much like finding a stated main idea. If you recall from Lesson 2, a main idea is defined as an assertion about the subject that controls or holds together all the ideas in the passage. Therefore, the main idea must be general enough to encompass all the ideas in the passage. Much like a net, it holds everything in the passage together. So far, all but one of the passages in this book have had a topic sentence that stated the main idea, so finding the main idea was something of a process of elimination: You could eliminate the sentences that weren't general enough to encompass the whole passage. But what do you do when there's no topic sentence?

You use your observations to make an inference—this time, an inference about the main idea or point of the passage.

▶ How to Find an Implied Main Idea

Finding an implied main idea requires you to use your observations to make an inference that, like a topic sentence, encompasses the whole passage. It might take a little detective work, but now that you know how to find details and how to understand word choice, style, and tone, you can make observations that will enable you to find main ideas even when they're not explicitly stated.

Practice Passage 1

For the first example of finding an implied main idea, let's look at a statement from a parking garage manager in response to recent thefts:

> Radios have been stolen from four cars in our parking garage this month. Each time, the thieves have managed to get by the parking garage security with radios in hand, even though they do not have a parking garage identification card, which people must show as they enter and exit the garage. Yet each time, the security officers say they have seen nothing unusual.

Now, there is no topic sentence in this paragraph, but you should be able to determine the main idea of this statement from the facts provided and from the tone. What does the statement suggest?

1. Which of the following best summarizes the statement's main idea?
   a. There are too many thefts in the garage.
   b. There are not enough security guards.
   c. There is something wrong with the security in the parking garage.

Answer

The correct answer is **c**, "There is something wrong with the security in the parking garage." How can you tell that this is the main idea? For one thing, it's the only one of the three choices general enough to serve as a "net" for the paragraph; choice **a** is implied only in the first sentence; and choice **b** isn't mentioned at all. In addition, each sentence on its own suggests that security in the parking garage has not been working properly. Furthermore, the word "yet" indicates that there is a conflict between the events that have taken place and the duties of the security officers.

Practice Passage 2

Now examine the following statement that a neighbor wrote about Mr. Miller, who owned one of the cars that was vandalized in the parking garage:

> Well, Mr. Miller's a pretty carefree person. I've borrowed his car on several occasions, and a few times, I've found the doors unlocked when I arrived at the garage. He often forgets things, too, like exactly where he parked the car on a particular day or where he put his keys. One time, I found him wandering around the garage looking for his keys, which he thought he dropped on the way to the car, and it turned out the car door was unlocked anyway. Sometimes, I wonder how he remembers his address, let alone to take care of his car.

2. What is Mr. Miller's neighbor suggesting?
   a. Mr. Miller forgets everything.
   b. Mr. Miller may have left his car door unlocked the day the radio was stolen.
   c. Mr. Miller is too carefree for his own good.

Answer

You can attack the question this way: Which of these three statements do the sentences in the neighbor's statement support? Try a process of elimination. Do all of the sentences support choice **a**? If not, cross **a** out. Do all of the sentences support choice **b**? Choice **c**?

The correct answer is **b**, "Mr. Miller may have left his car door unlocked the day the radio was stolen." How can you tell? Because this is the only idea that all of the sentences in the neighbor's statement support. You know that Mr. Miller often doesn't lock his car doors; you also know that he often forgets thing. The combination makes it likely that Mr. Miller left his car door unlocked on the day his car radio was stolen.

Practice Passage 3

Now look at a paragraph in which the *language* the writer uses is what enables you to determine meaning. Here is a description of Coach Lerner, a college basketball coach, written by one of his players. Read the paragraph carefully and see if you can determine the implied main idea of the paragraph.

> Coach Lerner, my basketball coach, is six feet ten inches tall with a voice that booms like a foghorn and the haircut of a drill sergeant. Every morning, he marches onto the basketball court at precisely 8:00 and dominates the gymnasium for the next three hours. He barks orders at us the entire time and expects that we will respond like troops on a battlefield. And if we fail to obey his commands, he makes us spend another 45 minutes under his rule.

Before you decide on the implied main idea, list your observations. What did you notice about the language in this paragraph? An example is provided to get you started.

Your Observations:

Example: *I noticed that Coach Lerner's voice is compared to a foghorn.*

3. Which of the following best expresses the implied message of the passage?
   a. Playing on Coach Lerner's team is difficult.
   b. Playing on Coach Lerner's team is like being under the command of an army general.
   c. Coach Lerner is a terrible basketball coach.

Answer

The correct answer is **b**, "Playing on Coach Lerner's team is like being under the command of an army general." There are many clues in the language of this paragraph that lead you to this inference. First, you probably noticed that Coach Lerner's voice "booms like a foghorn." This comparison (called a *simile*) suggests that Coach Lerner wants his voice to be heard and obeyed.

Second, the description of Coach Lerner's haircut is a critical part of the way the author establishes the tone of this paragraph. To say that he has "the haircut of a drill sergeant" (also a *simile*) makes us think of a military leader whose job it is to train soldiers. A writer wouldn't use this comparison unless he or she wanted to emphasize military-like discipline.

The author tells us that Coach Lerner "marches onto the basketball court," "barks orders," and expects his players to respond like "troops on a battlefield." The writer could have said that Coach Lerner "strides" onto the court, that he barks "instructions," and that he expects his players to act like "trained dogs." However, since the author is trying to paint a picture of Coach Lerner that will bring to mind a military leader, he uses words that convey military ideas. Thus, though answers **a** and **c** may be true—it *might* be difficult to play for Coach Lerner and he *might* be a terrible basketball coach—answer **b** is the only idea that all of the sentences in the paragraph support.

Of course, this person's description of Coach Lerner is very subjective, using as it does the first-person point of view. As an active reader, you should wonder whether everyone sees Coach Lerner this way or if this player is unable to be objective.

Practice Passage 4

Many people find reading literature a difficult task because in literature (fiction, drama, and poetry), the main idea is almost never expressed in a clear topic sentence. Instead, readers have to look for clues often hidden in the language of the text. For example, the following fictional paragraph describes a character. Read it carefully, make your observations, and then identify the main idea of the paragraph:

Every morning when Clara arrives at the gym, she is greeted with a buzz of warm hellos. She starts her workout in the weight room, where her exercise regimen is always peppered with lively chats with those around her. She then moves on to the pool, where she stops and converses with other friends and acquaintances before diving in and swimming laps. As she swims, her sole focus is the calming sound of her body gliding through the water—a rare moment in her always very social days.

Your Observations:

Example: *I noticed that Clara talks with many people.*

4. The main idea of this paragraph is that
  a. Clara is shy.
  b. Clara knows everyone at the gym.
  c. Clara is very friendly.

Answer

Although it is possible that **b**, "Clara knows everyone at the gym," there is no evidence in this paragraph to support that inference. Thus, **b** cannot be the main idea. Answer **a**, "Clara is shy," cannot be the correct answer either, since everything in the paragraph suggests that Clara is, in fact, quite outgoing.

Furthermore, the language of the paragraph creates a feeling of warmth and friendliness: Clara is greeted with "warm hellos" and she has "lively chats" and conversations with friends and acquaintances. She also has "very social days." All these words work together in the paragraph to paint a picture of someone who is very friendly and social. Thus, without directly saying so, the writer tells us that **c**, "Clara is very friendly."

▶ Summary

Many writers use implication to convey meaning rather than directly stating their ideas. This is especially true in literature, where readers generally prefer suggestion to direct statements. Finding the implied main idea requires a little detective work, but it is not as difficult as you may have thought, now that you know more about language and the way words can be used to suggest ideas.

Skill Building until Next Time

- Listen carefully to people today. Are there times when they *imply* things without directly saying them? Are there times when *you* use suggestion to get your ideas across? How do you do this? Be aware of how you and others use indirect language and suggestion to convey meaning.
- Write a paragraph that does not have a topic sentence. You should have a clear idea of the main idea before you write your paragraph and make sure your sentences use language that will help your readers understand your main idea. For example, think of a topic sentence about the kind of person you are, but don't write it down. Then, write several sentences that support your topic sentence with language that leads your reader to the proper conclusion. You may want to show your paragraph to others to see if they can correctly infer your main idea.

17 ▶ Assuming Causes and Predicting Effects

LESSON SUMMARY

Today's lesson focuses on how to determine cause and effect when they are only implied, rather than explicitly stated.

Have you ever regretted just "telling it like it is"? Many times, you can't come right out and say what you'd like, but like writers, you can get your ideas across through *implication* or inference.

This lesson focuses on two specific types of implication: reading between the lines to *determine cause* and reading between the lines to *predict effects*.

In case you need a reminder: A *cause* is the person or thing that makes something happen or produces an effect. An *effect* is the change that occurs as a result of some action or cause. Cause tells us why something happened; effect tells us what happened after a cause (or series of causes).

▶ Determining Implied Causes

In order to see how to determine causes that are implied rather than stated, look at the following brief fictional passage. Read the passage carefully and actively. After you make your observations, see if you can use the writer's clues to determine why the characters are fighting.

Anne sat with her feet up on the couch, drinking a Coke. She heard footsteps by the front door. Brenda was right on time, as usual. Never a minute early or late—for her, everything was very exact.

Anne placed her feet on the floor, reached for the remote, and turned off the television. She knew Brenda would demand her complete attention. She knew Brenda would hang up her coat in the closet by the door (third hanger from the left) and then head to the kitchen for her daily inspection (exactly seven steps). She knew this because they had been roommates for six months. Taking a deep breath, she thought about what she would say to Brenda. She waited and watched from her spot on the couch.

A moment later, Brenda stepped into the kitchen and surveyed the scene. Anne watched her expression, watched her eyes focus on the sink, and watched her face harden when she saw the dishes piled high. Pointing to the dishes, Brenda said disappointedly, "I don't believe what I'm seeing. I thought we agreed to share the responsibilities. I thought it was your turn to clean the kitchen this week?"

"I haven't gotten to them yet," Anne replied. "I've been really busy. Relax. I've got all night." She walked into the kitchen and added her empty glass to the top of the pile.

Brenda fumed. "You know I'm having company tonight! Somehow I thought you would have done your share in the kitchen. If we want to remain roommates, things have to change."

The phone rang, and Anne darted to answer it.

Brenda said in the background, "Tell them to call back, we need to settle this now. I told you I'm having company soon."

Anne ignored Brenda's comment and continued to engage in conversation with a good friend of hers. "Did I ever tell you about the time when . . ."

Look carefully at the dialogue between these two characters. What do they say to each other? How is it said? What other clues from the author can you find in this passage to help you understand the cause of their conflict? List your observations below and then answer the questions that follow.

Your Observations:

Example: *I noticed that Anne was relaxing and watching TV when Brenda arrived.*

1. Why does Brenda get angry?
   a. because Anne is unfriendly
   b. because she had a bad day at work
   c. because Anne didn't do the dishes
   d. because Anne is lazy

2. Why didn't Anne do the dishes?
   a. She didn't have time to do them.
   b. She wanted to start a fight.
   c. She was too lazy.
   d. She wants Brenda to get a new roommate.

3. What does Anne do that shows she doesn't intend to shoulder her share of the responsibilities?
   a. She turns off the television.
   b. She begins to wash the dishes in the sink.
   c. She always helps around the house.
   d. She talks on the phone with a good friend.

Answers

1. c. Brenda's face "hardens" with anger when she sees the dishes in the sink. You can tell she expects the kitchen to be clean when she comes home. Anne waits for Brenda to begin her "daily inspection," and when she walks in, she looks around the kitchen as if she's inspecting it. Then she sees the dishes and her face hardens. She asks why the dishes are still in the sink. Further, she reminds Anne about the company she is expecting.

2. b. You can tell Anne is not worried about Brenda's reaction because she is lazily watching television instead of cleaning the kitchen. She knows Brenda is going to check the kitchen and that Brenda is going to be mad about the dishes when she sees them. As Anne waits, she thinks about what she is going to say to Brenda.

3. d. Anne's actions speak loudly. She answers the phone and discontinues a conversation that is important if the two of them intend to remain roommates.

▶ Finding Implied Effects

Just as writers can imply cause, they can also suggest effects. In the practice passage you just read, Anne clearly had a specific goal. She purposely decided not to do the dishes in an act of rebellion. Why? You know a little bit about Anne and Brenda from the passage. Use that knowledge to answer the following question. What do you think Anne was hoping to achieve? What effect do you think she was looking for?

1. Brenda would do the dishes herself for once.
2. Brenda would get herself a new roommate.
3. Brenda would stop being so neat and so regimented.

How can you tell that number 3 is the best answer? You have to look carefully at the passage. Anne says, "Relax. I've got all night." But, Brenda has her own priorities. She says she is expecting company. Anne responds by ignoring her and turning to a phone conversation.

The passage doesn't directly say so, but from these clues, you can conclude that Anne's personality is clearly more relaxed than Brenda's. That's why she didn't do the dishes and that's also why she gladly took a phone call.

But will she get the effect she hoped for? Take another look at the passage, paying close attention to the end. What do you think? Will Anne get her wish? Will Brenda change her ways? Why do you think so?

Most likely, Anne won't get her wish. How can you tell? The end of the passage offers a strong clue. Brenda clearly wants to resolve the situation, but she can't compete with the telephone and probably not with Anne's relaxed personality.

▶ Determining Implied Effects

In order to learn how to determine implied effects, take another look at Mr. Miller (the man who had a radio stolen from his car) and the parking garage where he parks. Reread the statement of the parking garage manager as well as the one from Mr. Miller's neighbor and then use these statements to predict how the robbery will affect Mr. Miller and the parking garage.

Parking garage manager

Radios have been stolen from four cars in our parking garage this month. Each time, the thieves have managed to get by the parking garage security with radios in hand, even though they do not have a parking garage identification card, which people must show as they enter and exit the garage. Yet each time, the security officers say they have seen nothing unusual.

Mr. Miller's neighbor

Well, Mr. Miller's a pretty carefree person. I've borrowed his car on several occasions, and a few times, I've found the doors unlocked when I arrived at the garage. He often forgets things, too, like exactly where he parked the car on a particular day or where he put his keys. One time, I found him wandering around the garage looking for his keys, which he thought he dropped on the way to the car, and it turned out the car door was unlocked anyway. Sometimes, I wonder how he remembers his address, let alone to take care of his car.

Based on these two paragraphs, which of the following effects would be logical results (effects) of the thefts? Circle the correct answers.

1. Security will be tighter in the parking garage from now on.

2. People walking in and out of the garage will be required to show their identification cards with no exceptions.

3. The security officers will be fired.

4. Mr. Miller will get his radio back.

5. Mr. Miller will be more careful about locking his car door.

6. Mr. Miller will get a new car.

7. Some people who currently park in the garage will find a new garage to park their car.

8. Mr. Miller will be more careful with his keys.

Answers

Effects 1, 2, 5, 7, and 8 are logical predicted outcomes.

Effect 3 is not likely because it is too extreme; the parking garage manager's statement does not suggest that he plans to fire security guards. Rather, it suggests that he plans to look into the security problem.

There is nothing in either statement to suggest that effect 4 (that Mr. Miller will get his radio back) is correct.

Finally, there is no reason at all to think that Mr. Miller will get a new car because his radio was stolen. He'll likely get a new radio and perhaps he'll look for a new parking garage, but there's no evidence from the two statements to suggest that a new car is a likely possibility.

▶ Summary

In reading, particularly in reading literature, as well as in real life, you often have to figure out what the causes of a particular event or situation might have been. The same is true of effects: Both in reading and in life, you spend a lot of time trying to predict the outcomes of real or predicted actions or events. If you "read between the lines" without going too far beyond what the passage (or real-life event) actually contains, you can usually do a pretty good job of predicting these causes and effects.

Skill Building until Next Time

- Observe people's behavior today. If you see people acting particularly happy, sad, or angry, or exhibiting some other strong emotion or behavior, see if you can find any clues as to the cause of their emotion or behavior. Are they reading a letter? Talking with someone? Waiting for something? *Why* are they reacting this way?
- Read a news article today that discusses a current event—an election, a train crash, or a political scandal, for example. What effects can you predict will come about as a result of this event? Try to come up with at least three predictions based on what you read.

18 ▶ Emotional Versus Logical Appeals

LESSON SUMMARY

Writers often appeal to your emotions to try to persuade you of something. But unless they also provide logical evidence to back up their claims, you have no *reason* to accept their argument as valid. This lesson helps you see how to distinguish between appeals to your emotions and appeals to your sense of reason.

Imagine that you are about to do something when someone runs up to you and says, "You can't do that!"

"Why not?" you ask.

"Because! You just can't, that's all."

Now, "Because!" is not likely to convince you that you shouldn't do what you were about to do, is it? Why not? Well, "Because!" does not provide you with a *reason* for not doing what you wanted to do. It is not, therefore, a very convincing argument.

▶ The Difference between Logical and Emotional Appeals

When writers want to convince people of something or influence them to think a certain way, they generally rely on two means of persuasion: appealing to the reader's sense of logic and appealing to the reader's emotions. It is important to be able to distinguish between these two types of appeal because when writers rely *only* on appeals to emotion, they neglect to provide any real *evidence* for why you should believe what they say. Writers who rely solely on emotional appeals usually hope to get their readers so angry, scared, or excited that they will forget to look for reason or sense in the argument.

Unfortunately, many readers aren't aware of this strategy, so they may accept arguments that are unfounded, manipulative, or both. Political leaders who use the emotional strategy in speaking to crowds are called *demagogues*. Calling a leader a demagogue is no compliment since it means that he or she relies on prejudice and passion rather than clear thinking to persuade people of his or her position. Sound reasoning requires that you are able to look beyond emotional appeals to determine if there is any *logic* behind them.

> **Logical:** according to reason; according to conclusions drawn from evidence or good common sense
> **Emotional:** relating to emotions; arousing or exhibiting strong emotion

While it is true that an appeal to emotions can help *strengthen* an argument based in logic, an argument cannot be valid if it is based solely on emotional appeal.

▶ Distinguishing between Logical and Emotional Appeals

The best way to see the difference between logical and emotional appeals is to look at some examples. Actively read the passages that follow, trying to discern whether the author is appealing primarily to your sense of reason or to your emotions.

Practice Passage 1

The City Council of Ste. Jeanne should reject mandatory recycling. First, everyone knows that recycling doesn't really accomplish very much and that people who support it are mostly interested in making themselves *feel* better about the environment. They see more and more road construction and fewer and fewer trees and buy into the notion that sending bottles and cans to a recycling plant rather than a landfill will reverse the trend. Unfortunately, that notion is no more than wishful thinking.

Second, the proponents of mandatory recycling are the same people who supported the city's disastrous decision to require an increase in the number of public bus routes. After the mayor spent hundreds of thousands of dollars for the new buses and for street signs, bus shelters, and schedules, we all quickly learned that there was little to no interest in using public transportation among the people for whom the new routes were intended. Mandatory recycling would add yet another chapter to the book of wasteful government programs.

Finally, I'd like every citizen to answer this question in the privacy of his or her own heart: Would the mandatory recycling law really influence behavior? Or would most people, in fact, go on doing what they are doing now? That is, wouldn't the recyclers keep on recycling and the people who throw their bottles and cans in the trash continue to do just that (only being a little bit more careful, burying the bottles inside "legal" trash such as pizza boxes and coffee filters)? Why should any of us be forced to be surreptitious about something so simple as throwing away a soft drink can? I urge both the council and the mayor to reject this misguided proposal.

Chances are that no matter how you *feel* about mandatory recycling programs, this passage provoked a reaction in you. Perhaps you found some of the writer's arguments convincing; perhaps they simply made you want to argue back. But take another look at the passage. Is there any appeal to your sense of logic here—reason, evidence, or common sense? Or is the author only appealing to your preexisting ideas and feelings about environmentalism and government programs?

What Reasons Does the Writer Offer?

To help you see whether the writer's appeals are based on logic or emotion, break down his argument. The writer offers three different reasons for opposing the mandatory recycling proposal. List them here.

1.

2.

3.

You probably noticed that each of the three paragraphs deals with a different reason that the writer opposes the mandatory recycling program. They are:

1. Recycling programs do not help the environment and people who support the mandatory recycling program do so simply in order to make themselves feel better about a declining environment.

2. The people who support mandatory recycling also supported a failed program to increase city bus routes.

3. A mandatory recycling program would not actually cause people who do not presently recycle to begin recycling.

Are the Appeals Logical?

The next step is to see if these reasons are *logical*. Does the author come to these conclusions based on reason, evidence, or common sense? If you look carefully, you will see that the answer is *no*. Each of the writer's arguments is based purely on emotion without any logic to support it.

Begin with the first reason: *Recycling programs do not help the environment and people who support the mandatory recycling program do so simply in order to make themselves feel better about a declining environment.* Is there any logic behind this argument? Is this statement based on evidence, such as poll data showing a link between feeling bad about the environment and supporting the program, or environmental reports showing that recycling doesn't improve the environment to any appreciable degree?

Regardless of whether you agree or disagree with this author, you can probably see that this argument is based only in emotion rather than in logic. The argument crumbles when you break it down. The author tries to blunt any skepticism about his argument by saying that "everyone knows" that recycling doesn't accomplish very much and that people support it mostly for selfish reasons. He states this as if it was an established fact, but he fails to establish it with evidence. Even though many people may agree, no one can correctly claim that everyone knows this to be true—as presented, it is mere opinion. In fact, many people would argue in turn that recycling does a great deal to help clean up the environment. And if the writer cannot say for a fact that recycling doesn't work, how can he convincingly assert that people support it for selfish reasons?

Even without this flaw, the writer's argument is not logical because there is no evidence in this essay that the particular mandatory recycling program being discussed by the city council will not work. The author moves from stating his opposition to the program in the first sentence to a paragraph of unconvincing generalities about recycling programs in general.

The author's second argument is that *the people who support mandatory recycling also supported a failed program to increase city bus routes*. Is there any logic in this statement? No, not if we bear in mind that the point of the argument is the recycling program and not the bus route program. Readers who are sympathetic to the underlying message that many government programs are wasteful may get caught up in the emotion of their opinion and lose sight of the fact that the author is not even talking about the proposed mandatory recycling plan. The argument is designed to succeed by appealing to this underlying sympathetic response rather than by addressing the merits and demerits of the proposal being considered.

The third argument is that *a mandatory recycling program would not actually cause people who do not presently recycle to begin recycling*. Again, the author offers no evidence for his claim. Instead, he works on his readers' sense of shame about their own failure to comply with local ordinances or on their cynicism about whether their fellow citizens will comply with such rules. He doesn't offer evidence that people won't comply, or that the law enforcement authorities will be ineffective in forcing compliance, instead suggesting that the proposed program would be an undue burden, forcing good people to act "surreptitious," or stealthy, about everyday, innocent actions. Again, he avoids supporting his argument with logic, reason, or evidence.

Practice Passage 2

Now look at another argument for the same position. Notice how much more logical this essay is—whether you agree with the author—simply because the author gives explanations and evidence for his position rather than appealing solely to the readers' emotions.

The City Council of Ste. Jeanne should reject mandatory recycling. Although many good people support this idea, the proposal facing us is so deeply flawed that I believe their support is misplaced. The most glaring problem is that the mandatory recycling program proposed here would create at least as much pollution as it would eliminate. Our neighbors in Youngsville could testify to that: Greensleaves Recycling, the proposed contractor, got the recycling contract in Youngsville five years ago, and their machinery spewed so much toxic gas out of its smokestacks that the city government stopped all recycling, mandatory or optional, for a solid year.

One of the biggest concerns people have is that the bottles and cans they throw away today will either accumulate in unsightly, unsanitary landfills or go up in smoke from an incinerator. But the fact of the matter is that new waste treatment facilities in nearby counties soon will eliminate most of the need for landfills and incinerators. By compacting unsorted trash into blocks comparable in hardness to concrete, the new facilities make it available for use in building foundations, dikes, and road construction. This form of "recycling" — not part of the present proposal — doesn't require us to collect the garbage in any new way because it doesn't matter whether the content is coffee grounds or juice bottles.

An argument in favor of the recycling proposal for which I have some sympathy is that mandatory recycling will raise people's awareness of our beautiful and fragile environment. Reflecting on this, however, I recalled our wonderful educational programs, both in the schools and in the mass media. Voluntary recycling is at an all-time high level of participation; both anglers and environmentalists are celebrating the recent reopening of the Ste. Jeanne Waterway to fishing; downtown Ste. Jeanne won the "Greening of the State" award just last year. Taken together, these facts suggest to me a populace already deeply engaged with environmental issues and now looking hard for new, well-conceived proposals to do even more. The present proposal simply doesn't measure up to our city's high standards.

You probably noticed immediately that this passage also gives three reasons for not supporting the mandatory recycling program—so the authors don't differ over whether or not to reject the proposed program. The two passages don't have as much in common in their style of argument, though, and that is our focus here. Let's take a closer look at passage 2.

What Reasons Does the Writer Offer?

Break this argument down as you did the first one. Here are the reasons the author of passage 2 provides in arguing that the mandatory recycling program should be rejected. Underneath each reason, make a note about the *logic* behind the reason; say what reasoning, evidence, or common sense the author points to in support of the argument.

1. The proposed mandatory recycling program would cause as much pollution as it would eliminate.

2. New waste treatment facilities lessen the need for recycling programs.

3. The mandatory recycling program is not needed to raise people's awareness of the environment.

Are the Appeals Logical?

Whether you agree with the author, you can see that this is a much more effective argument because the writer uses logic and common sense in backing up what he has to say.

The first argument is supported in the following way:

- The proposed contractor caused a great deal of pollution from smokestacks in a nearby city five years before.
- The smokestack toxicity in the nearby city was so extensive that even voluntary recycling was halted for a year, meaning that even less recycling took place than before the mandatory recycling program began.

The second argument is supported by the following logic:

- New waste treatment facilities allow all waste to be reused without the need for sorting it into waste to be recycled and waste to be incinerated or put in a landfill, but the proposed plan does not involve these new facilities.

Finally, the third argument is supported this way:

- The populace of Ste. Jeanne is already highly conscious of the environment, and benefit for educational programs in the schools and the mass media.
- The high environment-consciousness of the people shows (a) the high rate of voluntary recycling, (b) the celebrated reopening of the Ste. Jeanne Waterway to fishing, and (c) the city's downtown winning a state environmental award the previous year.

More Practice

Now that you've examined two brief essays—one that appeals to emotion and one that appeals to logic—see if you can correctly identify the approaches used by the writers of the following sentences. Look carefully for a sense of logic. If the writer is appealing to your emotions, is the author's argument also backed up by logic (common sense, reason, or evidence)? Write an E in the blank if it appeals *only* to your sense of emotion and an L if it appeals to logic.

_____ **1.** Using a cell phone when driving is dangerous and anyone who does this is stupid.

_____ **2.** Using a cell phone when driving is dangerous because when drivers hold a cell phone to their ear, they're only using one hand to control their motor vehicle, which makes them much more likely to have an accident.

_____ **3.** Many states have banned cell phone use when driving because it is dangerous. These laws have been put into effect because of startling statistics that point to the elevated risk of car accidents due to cell phone use.

_____ **4.** Dogs should always be kept on a leash in public places. What if you were walking down the street minding your own business and a loose dog ran up and attacked you?

_____ **5.** Dogs should always be kept on a leash in public places. A leash can protect dogs from traffic, garbage, dangerous places, and getting lost. It can also protect people from being harmed by overzealous, angry, or agitated dogs.

Answers

It should be clear that argument 1 is an appeal to emotion without any logic and that arguments 2, 3, and 5 use common sense, evidence, and reason. But argument 4 might not be so obvious since it may seem like a reasonable argument. However, it does not address all the logical reasons that leashes are necessary but instead points to one frightening possibility. Yes, we would all like to avoid being attacked by a dog, which is a scary and threatening possibility, and by using only this scenario in the argument, the writer is appealing directly to our emotions.

▶ Summary

Looking for appeals to logic will make you a more critical reader and thinker. And once you learn to read between the lines in an argument (to look behind emotional appeals for some sort of logical support), you'll have more confidence as a reader and be a better judge of the arguments that you hear and read.

Skill Building until Next Time

- Listen carefully to how people around you try to convince you (or others) when they want you to think or act a certain way. For example, if a friend wants you to try a new place for lunch, how does he or she try to convince you: with appeals to your sense of logic ("The food is great—and so are the prices!") or to your emotions ("What, are you afraid to try something new?")? If your boss asks you to work overtime, does he or she appeal to your sense of logic ("You'll make lots of extra money") or to your emotions ("I could really, really use your help")? See which arguments you find most convincing and why.
- Read an editorial from the Opinion-Editorial page of your local newspaper. Look at how the writer supports his or her argument. Is the editiorial convincing? Why? What reasons or evidence does it use to support its position?

19 ▶ Finding Meaning in Literature

LESSON SUMMARY

Many people are scared of reading literature—stories, poems, and plays—especially if they have to answer questions about it, as in a test situation. But now that you know so much about finding an implied main idea, you can also find the *theme,* or main idea, of a work of literature. This lesson works with poetry to show you how to do it.

Literature (novels, poems, stories, and plays) can be quite intimidating to many readers. In literature, meanings are often implied, and messages and themes are not conveniently housed in a topic sentence. However, no matter what you are reading, you can feel confident that the author has left behind clues that will help you to find the theme (*the main idea*). As an active reader, you are now well-equipped to read between the lines to find meaning in anything you read.

Throughout these pages, you have spent a great deal of time locating the main ideas in various pieces of writing. Finding the theme of a work of literature is similar to finding the main idea in an article, passage, or memo. Just as the main idea is more than the subject of a given article, passage, or memo, the theme of a work of literature is also more than just its subject: It is what the text says *about* that subject. Theme, in other words, is the overall message or idea that a work of literature conveys. For example, you can probably figure out from the title that the *subject* of John Donne's poem "Death Be Not Proud" is death. However, the *theme* is not merely "death," but what the poem says *about* death, which happens to be that death is a gift if one believes in God.

There isn't room in this short lesson to look at theme in a short story, novel, or play. So this lesson will introduce you to a few poems. But don't be frightened: Reading poetry is really just like reading anything else. You just have to read a little more carefully and rely a little more on your sense of observation. You find theme in poetry the same way you do in other kinds of writing: by looking for clues in what happens and in the words the writer uses to describe what happens.

▶ How Action Conveys Theme

First, look at an example of how the action of a poem—what happens in it—leads you to understand the theme.

Practice Passage 1

Read the following poem by William Blake from his book *Songs of Experience,* published in 1794. Read it out loud, because poetry is meant to be *heard* as well as read. Then read it again with your pen in hand: Read actively, making your observations and comments in the margins. Then answer the questions that follow.

A Poison Tree

I was angry with my friend;
I told my wrath, my wrath did end.   *wrath = anger*
I was angry with my foe: *foe = enemy*
I told it not, my wrath did grow.

And I water'd it in fears,
Night & morning with my tears;
And I sunned it with smiles,
And with soft deceitful wiles.   *wiles = trickery, deceit*

And it grew both day and night,
Till it bore an apple bright;
And my foe beheld it shine,
And he knew that it was mine.

And into my garden stole
When the night had veil'd the pole: *veiled = concealed*
In the morning glad I see
My foe outstretch'd beneath the tree.

What Happened?

To understand the author's theme, you need to look carefully at what happened, and why. Look at each of the four stanzas (a stanza is a poetic "paragraph"; each stanza in this poem is four lines long) to track the action.

What happens in the first stanza?

1. The speaker was angry with
   a. a friend.
   b. a foe.
   c. his friend and his foe.

2. How did the speaker handle his anger toward his friend?
   a. He told his friend about it and it went away.
   b. He kept it to himself and it grew.
   c. He kept it to himself and it went away.

3. How did the speaker handle his anger toward his foe?
   a. He told his friend about it and it went away.
   b. He kept it to himself and it grew.
   c. He kept it to himself and it went away.

You probably figured out the answers without too much trouble: **1. c, 2. a, 3. b.**

Now look at the second stanza. The key to understanding this stanza is knowing what "it" refers to. Reread the first and second stanzas carefully in order to answer the next question.

4. "It" refers to
   a. tears.
   b. smiles.
   c. wrath.

Choice **c**—"wrath"—is the last thing mentioned in the first stanza, so it follows that "wrath" is what "it" refers to.

The second stanza tells us that the speaker "water'd" it (his wrath) with fears and "sunned" it with smiles and wiles. How can this be? Can you literally water and sun your anger? No, but the speaker is not being literal here. Instead, he is using figurative language. Like the similes we saw earlier about Coach Lerner, comparing his voice to a foghorn and his haircut to that of a drill sergeant, this stanza uses a *metaphor*—a comparison that doesn't use the words *like* or *as*—to compare the speaker's wrath to something that grows with water and sun. Now, given these clues (and the best clue of all, the title of the poem), to what exactly is the speaker comparing his wrath?

5. The speaker compares his wrath to
   a. a flower.
   b. a tree.
   c. the sun.

The answer, of course, is **b**, a tree. The title gives this away. Also, a tree is the only plant that could bear "an apple bright," as in the third stanza.

What else happens in the third stanza?

6. In the third stanza, the foe
   a. grows his own apple.
   b. shines the speaker's apple.
   c. sees the speaker's apple.

The answer is **c**, the foe sees the speaker's apple ("my foe beheld it shine").

Finally, what happens in the fourth stanza? This stanza is somewhat trickier than the others, because in this stanza, something happens that is not directly stated. You know that the foe sneaks into the speaker's garden ("And into my garden stole"), but what else happens?

The poem doesn't exactly tell you, but you can guess. The speaker had an apple; you know that this apple grew on a tree and that this tree is a metaphor for the speaker's anger. You also know that the poem is called "A Poison Tree." You read in the fourth stanza that, in the morning, the speaker finds his foe "outstretch'd beneath the tree." What can you conclude?

7. At the end of the fourth stanza, the foe
   a. is waiting to ambush the speaker and kill him with the apple.
   b. has been killed by the apple he stole because it was poisonous.
   c. is waiting to share the apple with the speaker.

Which answer do your clues add up to? The only one that can be correct is **b**. The speaker was angry; the tree (and so the apple) was poisonous. You know that the foe, seeing the apple, snuck into the speaker's garden. Apparently he ate the apple, because now he's "outstretch'd beneath the tree." You also know that the speaker is "glad" to see his foe outstretched this way—he's glad to see him dead.

What Does It Mean?

Okay, so that's what happened in the poem. But what does it all mean?

Look again at the action. What the speaker *did* was to tell his friend about his wrath. What the speaker *didn't* do was to tell his enemy about his wrath. The results of the speaker's action and his inaction are your clues to the meaning of the poem as a whole, its theme.

8. Which of the following best summarizes the theme of the poem?
   a. Don't steal; it can kill you.
   b. Choose your enemies carefully.
   c. If you don't talk about your anger, it can be deadly.

Before you go any further, think about your answer again. Like a main idea, a theme must be general enough to encompass the whole work, not just a piece of it. Does the answer you chose encompass the whole poem and not just part of it?

You should have chosen answer **c**, for this is the idea that sums up the message or "lesson" of the poem. In the first two lines, the speaker's wrath for his friend vanished when he talked about it, but he did not talk about his wrath for his enemy. Instead, he let it grow until it was poisonous and deadly.

► How Language Conveys Emotion

In addition to conveying a theme, poems also often use language to create a powerful image or emotion. After looking at how poets use language to convey an emotion or a picture, you'll be ready to put your understanding of the action and the language together to understand the meaning of a poem.

Practice Passage 2

Take a look at the following poem by British poet Alfred Lord Tennyson as an example of how language can convey a strong feeling by conveying an image or picture. Read "The Eagle" twice out loud—remember, poetry is meant to be heard, not just seen. Then mark it up and write your observations in the margin.

The Eagle

He clasps the crag with crooked hands;   *crag = steep*
Close to the sun in lonely lands,   *or rugged rock*
Ringed with the azure world, he stands.   *azure = sky blue*

The wrinkled sea beneath him crawls;
He watches from his mountain walls,
And like a thunderbolt he falls.

The Sound of Words

What did you notice about the language in this poem? Did you notice the rhyme in each stanza—*hands, lands, stands* and *crawls, walls, falls*? Did you notice the repetition of the "k" sound in *clasps, crag,* and *crooked*? This repetition of sounds (especially at the beginning of words) is called *alliteration*.

9. Which other line of this poem uses alliteration?
   a. line 2
   b. line 3
   c. line 6

The answer is line 2, which repeats the *l* sound in "*lonely lands*."

Picture Language

You may have noticed another poetic device at work in this poem. In line 1, the poet tells us that the eagle ("he") "clasps" the rock "with crooked hands." Do eagles have hands? No, they do not; but Tennyson gives the eagle human characteristics. When an animal is given human characteristics, or when a inanimate thing (like a rock, for example) is given animate characteristics (human or animal), it is called *personification*.

10. Which other line of this poem uses personification?
   a. line 2
   b. line 4
   c. line 6

The other example of personification is found in line 4, where the sea "crawls" like a baby or a turtle.

Here's a memory test:

11. Line 6, "And like a thunderbolt he falls," uses which of the following poetic devices?
   a. personification
   b. simile
   c. irony

This line uses **b**, a simile that compares the eagle to a thunderbolt. What is the effect of this comparison?

12. The comparison of the eagle to a thunderbolt makes the reader think of the eagle as
   a. a weak, timid creature.
   b. an unpredictable creature.
   c. a powerful, fast creature.

Like all good similes, this comparison creates a vivid image that not only helps us actually picture the eagle's flight, but also tells us *something about* the eagle by comparing it to the incredible force of nature that is lightning. The eagle, this simile suggests, is as powerful, as fast, as dangerous—and as impossible to catch—as a thunderbolt. We should, in short, be as awed by the eagle as we are by lightning—and that feeling, more than an idea we might call a theme, is what this poem is all about.

▶ Action + Language = Theme

In the final poem for today, by American poet Stephen Crane, see if you can determine the theme of the poem by looking at both the action of the poem and its language (diction, style, and tone). As before, begin by reading the poem carefully, first out loud and then with pen in hand.

Practice Passage 3

A Man Said to the Universe

A man said to the universe:
"Sir, I exist!"
"However," replied the universe,
"The fact has not created in me
A sense of obligation."

13. Which sentence best summarizes the theme of this poem?
   a. The universe is too big for humanity.
   b. The universe is indifferent to humanity.
   c. Humanity has an obligation to the universe.

The best answer is **b**, "The universe is indifferent to humanity." This idea is conveyed in part by the action of the poem: what the man says to the universe and the universe's reply. But the universe's indifference is also reflected in the language of the poem.

14. Which of the following best describes the tone of this poem?
   a. warm, caring
   b. hot, angry
   c. cold, formal

The words of this poem—especially "sir," "fact," and "sense of obligation"—are cold, formal words that reflect the way the universe feels about man: indifferent. There is no sense of intimacy, no relationship, no warmth in these words. The poet's diction and style help to reveal the theme of the poem.

▶ Summary

Reading poetry wasn't so bad after all, was it? If you are an active reader who is sensitive to the language used by the poet, you can use the clues the poet gives you to help you enjoy the pictures and emotions created through words and understand the poem's theme. And if you can do this for poems, you can certainly do it for stories, novels, and plays as well.

Skill Building until Next Time

- Read a poem on your own today. See if you can read between the lines to determine its theme.
- Read a short story today. Apply the techniques you used to determine the theme in a poem to determine the theme of the story.

20

Drawing Conclusions: Putting It All Together

LESSON SUMMARY

This lesson wraps up your study of reading comprehension by reviewing everything you've learned so far.

Y ou're almost at the end of this book. If you've been doing a lesson every weekday, you've spent almost a month building your reading skills. Congratulations! This lesson uses a longer passage than the ones you've read so far to give you a chance to practice all the skills you've learned. Here's a quick review of what you've learned since the last review lesson:

- **Lesson 16: Finding an implied main idea.** You practiced looking for clues in structure, language, and style, as well as the facts of the passage, to determine the main idea.
- **Lesson 17: Understanding implied causes and effects.** You learned to "read between the lines" to determine causes and make predictions about effects.
- **Lesson 18: Emotional and logical appeals.** You learned that arguments that appeal to readers' emotions must be supported by logic, as well in order, to be convincing.
- **Lesson 19: Finding the theme in literature.** You used your detective skills to find the main idea implied by the structure, language, style, and action in a work of literature.

If any of these terms or strategies sound unfamiliar to you, STOP. Please take a few minutes to review whatever lesson is unclear.

▶ Practice

Today, you'll practice these skills in combination with skills covered earlier in this book:

- Finding the facts
- Determining the main idea
- Determining the meaning of unfamiliar words
- Distinguishing between fact and opinion
- Chronological order
- Order of importance
- Cause and effect
- Comparison and contrast
- Point of view
- Diction
- Language and style
- Tone

If this seems like a monumental task, don't worry: It isn't. You've already mastered some of these skills and should be very comfortable with the others. In fact, you will probably be surprised at how easy you find this exercise to be.

Practice Passage

Are you ready? Read the following essay. Remember, read actively and make observations in the space provided on the next page. Then answer the questions that follow. This will give you a chance to see how well your reading skills are coming along.

Although many companies offer tuition reimbursement, most companies only reimburse employees for classes that are relevant to their position. This is a very limiting policy. A company that reimburses employees for all college credit courses—whether job related or not—offers a service not only to the employees, but to the entire company.

One good reason for giving employees unconditional tuition reimbursement is that it shows the company's dedication to its employees. In today's economy, where job security is a thing of the past and employees feel more and more expendable, it is important for a company to demonstrate to its employees that it cares. The best way to do this is with concrete investments in them.

In turn, this dedication to the betterment of company employees will create greater employee loyalty. A company that puts out funds to pay for the education of its employees will get its money back by having employees stay with the company longer. It will reduce employee turnover, because even employees who don't take advantage of the tuition reimbursement program will be more loyal to their company just knowing that their company cares enough to pay for their education.

Most importantly, the company that has an unrestricted tuition reimbursement program will have higher quality employees. Although these companies do indeed run the risk of losing money on employees who go on to another job in a different company as soon as they get their degree, more often than not, the employee will stay with the company. And even if employees do leave after graduation, it generally takes several years to complete any degree program. Thus, even if the employee leaves upon graduating, throughout those years, the employer will have a more sophisticated, more intelligent, and therefore more valuable and productive employee. And, if the employee stays, that education will doubly benefit the company: Not only is the employee more educated, but now that employee can be promoted so the company doesn't have to fill a high-level vacancy from the outside. Open positions can be filled by people who already know the company well.

Though unconditional tuition reimbursement requires a significant investment on the employer's part, it is perhaps one of the wisest investments a company can make.

Your Observations

Record your observations about the passage in the space below.

Questions

1. According to the passage, unconditional tuition reimbursement is good for which of the following reasons?
a. Employees get a cheaper education.
b. Employees become more valuable.
c. Employees can find better jobs.

2. How, according to the passage, will unconditional tuition reimbursement reduce employee turnover?
a. by making employees more loyal
b. by paying employees more money
c. by promoting education

3. The first sentence of the passage, "Although many companies offer tuition reimbursement, most companies only reimburse employees for classes that are relevant to their position," is
a. fact.
b. opinion.

4. The second sentence of the passage, "This is a very limiting policy," is
a. fact.
b. opinion.

5. This passage is organized according to which of the following strategies? (Mark all that apply.)
a. chronological order
b. order of importance
c. cause and effect
d. compare and contrast

6. The point of view used in this passage is the
a. first-person point of view.
b. second-person point of view.
c. third-person point of view.

7. The writer most likely chose this point of view because
a. the writer is describing a personal experience.
b. it enables readers to identify with the situation.
c. its objectivity encourages the reader to take the writer's ideas seriously.

8. The writer most likely uses the word *wisest* in the last sentence, rather than words such as *profitable, practical,* or *beneficial* because
a. wisdom is associated with education, the subject of the essay.
b. the writer trying to appeal to people who are already highly educated.

9. Which of the following words best describes the tone of this essay?
a. playful
b. optimistic
c. insincere

10. The passage suggests that, compared to employees of companies that offer unconditional tuition reimbursement, employees of companies that do not offer this benefit are
  a. less loyal.
  b. more likely to be promoted.
  c. not as smart.

11. "Expendable" (paragraph 2) most nearly means
  a. expensive.
  b. flexible.
  c. replaceable.

12. The writer appeals primarily to the reader's
  a. emotions.
  b. sense of logic.

13. The main idea of the passage is that
  a. companies should reimburse employees for work-related courses.
  b. both companies and employees would benefit from unconditional tuition reimbursement.
  c. companies should require their employees to take college courses.

Answers

1. b. The idea that employees will become more valuable if they take courses is stated in the fourth paragraph: "Thus . . . the employer will have a more sophisticated, more intelligent, and therefore more valuable and productive employee."

2. a. The idea that employees will become more loyal is stated in the third paragraph: "A company that puts out funds to pay for the education of its employees will get its money back by having employees stay with the company longer. It will reduce employee turnover because even employees who don't take advantage of the tuition reimbursement program will be more loyal . . ."

3. a. The sentence is a fact; you could verify it by surveying companies to find out about their tuition reimbursement policies.

4. b. The sentence is an opinion; it shows how the author feels about the policy.

5. b, c. The author lists the ways companies would benefit by having unconditional tuition reimbursement in order of importance from least to most important. The author also shows the positive effects unconditional reimbursement would have on the company.

6. c. There is no *I* or *you* here; the writer doesn't refer directly to herself or to the reader. Instead, everything is spoken of in the third person.

7. c. The writer most likely uses the third-person point of view because it is objective, and her argument is more likely to be taken seriously. If she used the first person, readers might think she was an employee who wanted her employer to pay for her tuition, and she wouldn't be taken seriously.

8. a. By using a word associated with education, the writer stresses the importance of education for the company.

9. b. The passage describes only positive effects of unconditional reimbursement; there is scarcely a negative word.

10. a. If employees of companies that offer unconditional tuition reimbursement are more loyal to their companies (see the second and third paragraphs), it follows that other employees will be less loyal because their company isn't showing enough dedication to their betterment.

11. c. Your best clue that *expendable* means *replaceable* is that the writer uses the word immediately after saying that job security is a thing of the past, so that workers don't feel they are important or valuable to a company that can fire them on a moment's notice.

12. b. There is common sense or reason behind each of the writer's arguments. Indeed, there are few, if any, emotional appeals in this passage.

13. b. This main idea is explicitly stated in the last sentence of the first paragraph (a good place to look for the main idea of a longer passage like this one) and repeated at the end of the passage.

How did you do? If you got all of the answers correct, congratulations! Good work. If you missed a few, you might want to take time to review the corresponding lessons.

IF YOU MISSED:	THEN STUDY:
Question 1	Lesson 1
Question 2	Lesson 1
Question 3	Lesson 4
Question 4	Lesson 4
Question 5	Lessons 6–10
Question 6	Lesson 11
Question 7	Lesson 11
Question 8	Lesson 12
Question 9	Lesson 14
Question 10	Lessons 16 and 17
Question 11	Lesson 3
Question 12	Lesson 18
Question 13	Lessons 2 and 16

▶ Congratulations!

You've completed 20 lessons and have seen your reading skills increase. If you're preparing for a standardized test, you should check out Appendix A, which provides tips on how to prepare and what to do during the test. And don't forget Appendix B, which gives suggestions for how to continue to improve your reading skills, along with a list of suggested books organized by subject categories.

Now it's time to reward yourself for a job well done. Buy yourself a good book and enjoy!

Posttest ▶

Now that you've spent a good deal of time improving your reading comprehension, take this posttest to see how much you've learned. If you took the pretest at the beginning of this book, you can compare what you knew when you started the book with what you know now.

When you complete this test, grade yourself, and then compare your score with your score on the pretest. If your score now is much greater than your pretest score, congratulations—you've profited noticeably from your hard work. If your score shows little improvement, perhaps you need to review certain chapters. Do you notice a pattern to the types of questions you got wrong? Whatever you score on this posttest, keep this book around for review and refer to it when you need tips on how to read more efficiently.

Use the answer sheet on the next page to fill in the correct answers. Or, if you prefer, simply circle the answer numbers in this book. If the book doesn't belong to you, write the numbers 1–50 on a piece of paper and record your answers there. Take as much time as you need to do this short test. When you finish, check your answers against the answer key that follows. Each answer tells you which lesson of this book teaches you about the reading strategy in that question.

1.	a	b	c	d		18.	a	b	c	d		35.	a	b	c	d
2.	a	b	c	d		19.	a	b	c	d		36.	a	b	c	d
3.	a	b	c	d		20.	a	b	c	d		37.	a	b	c	d
4.	a	b	c	d		21.	a	b	c	d		38.	a	b	c	d
5.	a	b	c	d		22.	a	b	c	d		39.	a	b	c	d
6.	a	b	c	d		23.	a	b	c	d		40.	a	b	c	d
7.	a	b	c	d		24.	a	b	c	d		41.	a	b	c	d
8.	a	b	c	d		25.	a	b	c	d		42.	a	b	c	d
9.	a	b	c	d		26.	a	b	c	d		43.	a	b	c	d
10.	a	b	c	d		27.	a	b	c	d		44.	a	b	c	d
11.	a	b	c	d		28.	a	b	c	d		45.	a	b	c	d
12.	a	b	c	d		29.	a	b	c	d		46.	a	b	c	d
13.	a	b	c	d		30.	a	b	c	d		47.	a	b	c	d
14.	a	b	c	d		31.	a	b	c	d		48.	a	b	c	d
15.	a	b	c	d		32.	a	b	c	d		49.	a	b	c	d
16.	a	b	c	d		33.	a	b	c	d		50.	a	b	c	d
17.	a	b	c	d		34.	a	b	c	d						

▶ Posttest

The posttest consists of a series of reading passages with questions that follow to test your comprehension.

Grunge Music and American Popular Culture

The late 1980s found the landscape of popular music in America dominated by a distinctive style of rock and roll known as *Glam Rock* or *Hair Metal*—so called because of the over-styled hair, makeup, and wardrobe worn by the genre's ostentatious rockers. Bands like Poison, Whitesnake, and Mötley Crüe popularized glam rock with their power ballads and flashy style, but the product had worn thin by the early 1990s. Just as superficial as the 80s, glam rockers were shallow, short on substance, and musically inferior.

In 1991, a Seattle-based band called Nirvana shocked the corporate music industry with the release of its debut single, "Smells Like Teen Spirit," which quickly became a huge hit all over the world. Nirvana's distorted, guitar-laden sound and thought-provoking lyrics were the antithesis of glam rock, and the youth of America were quick to pledge their allegiance to the brand-new movement known as *grunge*.

Grunge actually got its start in the Pacific Northwest during the mid-1980s. Nirvana had simply mainstreamed a sound and culture that got its start years before with bands like Mudhoney, Soundgarden, and Green River. Grunge rockers derived their fashion sense from the youth culture of the Pacific Northwest: a melding of punk rock style and outdoors clothing like flannels, heavy boots, worn out jeans, and corduroys. At the height of the movement's popularity, when other Seattle bands like Pearl Jam and Alice in Chains were all the rage, the trappings of grunge were working their way to the height of American fashion. Like the music, the teenagers were fast to embrace the grunge fashion because it represented defiance against corporate America and shallow pop culture.

The popularity of grunge music was ephemeral; by the mid- to late-1990s, its influence upon American culture had all but disappeared, and most of its recognizable bands were nowhere to be seen on the charts. The heavy sound and themes of grunge were replaced on the radio waves by boy bands like the Backstreet Boys, and the bubblegum pop of Britney Spears and Christina Aguilera.

There are many reasons why the Seattle sound faded out of the mainstream as quickly as it rocketed to prominence, but the most glaring reason lies at the defiant, anti-establishment heart of the grunge movement itself. It is very hard to buck the trend when you are the one setting it, and many of the grunge bands were never comfortable with the fame that was thrust upon them. Ultimately, the simple fact that many grunge bands were so against mainstream rock stardom eventually took the movement back to where it started: underground. The fickle American mainstream public, as quick as they were to hop on to the grunge bandwagon, were just as quick to hop off and move on to something else.

1. The word "ostentatious" in the first sentence most nearly means
   a. stubborn.
   b. youthful.
   c. showy.
   d. unadorned.

2. Teenagers embraced grunge fashion because
   a. they were tired of Glam Rock fashion.
   b. it defied corporate America and the shallowness of pop culture.
   c. grunge rockers told them to embrace it.
   d. it outraged their parents.

3. By stating that "glam rockers were shallow, short on substance, and musically inferior," this author is
   a. using a time-honored form of reporting that dignifies his or her position.
   b. resorting to a subjective, emotional assertion that is not an effective way to build an argument.
   c. making an objective, logical assertion based on facts.
   d. merely quoting what others say about glam rock and detaching her- or himself from the opinion.

4. This writer is trying to document
   a. the popularity of glam rock.
   b. Nirvana's role in popularizing grunge music.
   c. the rise and fall of grunge music.
   d. the reasons young people responded so enthusiastically to grunge music.

5. According to this passage, what is the difference between glam rock and grunge?
   a. Glam rock is flashier and superficial, while grunge is thought-provoking and anti-establishment.
   b. Glam rock appeals to teenagers, while grunge appeals to adults.
   c. Glam rock faded quickly, while grunge is still prominent.
   d. Glam rock was more commercially successful than grunge.

6. The tone of the sentence, "The fickle American mainstream public, as quick as they were to hop on to the grunge bandwagon, were just as quick to hop off and move on to something else" can be best described as
   a. authoritative.
   b. gloomy.
   c. cynical.
   d. ironic.

7. Which of the following bands is not associated with grunge?
   a. Nirvana
   b. Mudhoney
   c. Pearl Jam
   d. Backstreet Boys

To Lease or Not to Lease

Planning to lease a car because you don't think you can afford to buy? Think again. Leasing can end up being just as expensive as buying—and you don't even get to the keep the car. Most people who are thinking about leasing are attracted to this option because they believe it will cost them less money. And they're right—it is cheaper, but only in the short term. For example, if you were to lease a brand-new Subaru Forester with $4,000 down, you might pay $300 per month for the car. If you were to buy the same car with $3,000 down, you would pay closer to $400 per month. Over a three-year lease, that's $3,600—a big savings. But after your lease is over, you have to give the car back. If you want to keep driving, you'll either have to put another down-payment on another lease, or, if you have the option to buy the car, you'll have to pay thousands of dollars to purchase the vehicle—dollars that won't be spread out in more manageable monthly payments.

Many people want to lease because they can drive a more upmarket car than they might otherwise be able to afford. For example, if your monthly budget allowed you to spend $300 on a car, you might be able to lease a brand new Ford Explorer. For the same price, you might have to buy an Explorer that was two or three years old with 50,000 miles, or buy a new but considerably less expensive make and model. A lease, therefore, allows you to drive the latest models of more expensive cars. But when your lease is over, you will have to return that Explorer. Whatever car you can afford to buy, you get to keep it, and it will always have a resell or trade-in value if you want to later upgrade to a newer car.

Furthermore, people who lease cars are often shocked and appalled by how much they must pay when the lease is over. Most leases limit you to a certain number of miles, and if you go over that allotment, you must pay for each mile. As a result, at the end of a lease, you may end up paying thousands of dollars in mileage fees. For example, if your lease covers you for 25,000 miles over three years, but you drive 40,000, that's an extra 15,000 miles. At $.11 per mile, that's $1,650 you'll have to pay. And you still won't have a car.

In addition, when you lease, you still have to pay for regular maintenance and repairs to the vehicle. Since you must return the car when your lease expires, you are paying to repair someone else's car. If you own the car, however, you would know that every dollar you spend maintaining or repairing the car is an investment in a real piece of property—your property, not someone else's.

By now, the benefits of buying over leasing should be clear. But if you're still not convinced, remember this fundamental fact: If you lease, when your lease is up, and after you've made all of your monthly payments, paid for extra mileage, and paid for repairs, *you must give the car back.* It isn't yours to keep, no matter how much the lease cost you. Whatever make or model you can afford to buy, it is yours to keep after you make the payments. There's no giving it back, and that makes all the difference.

8. According to the passage, which of the following statements is true?
- **a.** People believe leasing will cost them less money.
- **b.** Most Americans lease rather than buy cars.
- **c.** Most car leases allow for unlimited mileage.
- **d.** Leasing a car is never as expensive as buying.

9. Which of the following sentences best summarizes the main idea of this passage?
- **a.** Leasing a car is a bad idea.
- **b.** The benefits of buying a car outweigh the benefits of leasing a car.
- **c.** Leasing allows people to drive more expensive cars than they might otherwise be able to afford.
- **d.** People are often shocked at how much money they end up paying when a car lease is over.

10. The author makes his or her point by
   a. making an argument using chronological order.
   b. arguing the benefits of buying from the most to least important.
   c. comparing and contrasting leasing and buying.
   d. stating opinions.

11. This writer bases his or her argument primarily on
   a. facts derived from the author's personal observations.
   b. opinions that others have reported to the author.
   c. facts with logic and statistics supporting them.
   d. opinions derived from the author's personal observations.

12. In another version of this passage, the first sentence of the third paragraph did not use the words "shocked and appalled" to describe the reaction of car leasers to how much money they must pay when the lease is over. Instead, the sentence read: "Furthermore, people who lease cars are usually unaware of how much they must pay when the lease is over." Why do you think the writer changed the sentence to include "shocked and appalled"?
   a. Someone he or she interviewed for the story used these words.
   b. These words make the author sound smarter.
   c. These words have a positive connotation that help the author make his or her case.
   d. These words have a powerful negative connotation that add to the author's arguments about the downfalls of leasing.

13. From the context, it can be determined that the word "upmarket" in the third paragraph means
   a. safer.
   b. bigger.
   c. expensive.
   d. dependable.

14. Why did the author choose the second-person point of view for this passage?
   a. The second-person point of view puts readers into the action of the writing.
   b. The second-person point of view makes readers imagine themselves in the situation.
   c. The second-person point of view makes readers pay more attention.
   d. all of the above

15. When this author says that "most people want to lease because they can then drive a more upmarket car," he or she is
   a. making a generalization that requires evidence before it can be confirmed.
   b. making an obvious generalization that needs no evidence.
   c. reaching an unreasonable conclusion based on evidence provided.
   d. reaching a reasonable conclusion based on evidence provided.

"The Weekly Visit"
(short story excerpt)

The requisite visit happened typically on sunny Saturdays, when my child spirits were at their highest and could be most diminished by the cramped interior of her house. My mother, accustomed to the bright, spacious farmhouse that was once Grandma's seemed no less susceptible to the gloom. She would set her jaw as Grandma described the many ailments attendant on age and would check her watch—an hour being the minimum she expected herself to withstand. Her barely contained impatience and my grandmother's crippling age radiated out around me. We were the women of the Carlson clan, each throbbing with agitation, like concentric, blinking circles on a radar screen.

I would sit at the white and red metal table with the pull-out leaves and built-in silverware drawer, cracking almonds. This was the one good thing at Grandma's house, the almonds, which she kept in a green Depression glass bowl. I would lift the lid carefully and try to set it down on the metal table quietly, then attempt to crack the nuts without scattering the shell crumbs. It was not good to draw attention to myself at Grandma Carlson's. Sounding angry, she would call to me in her croupy drawl. When I failed to understand her, she would reach out to me with her palsied, slick, wrinkled hand and shout, "Here!" She would be offering some of her horehound candy, which tasted like a cross between butterscotch and bitter sticks.

There was this lamentable air in the dim house with its itchy mohair furniture and its dark colors, an awareness—Grandma's—underlying the mentholatum, that her age scared her grandkids. I would yearn during the dutiful visit to get outside into the yard, where Grandma had transplanted a few flowers when she moved from the farm. But even the yard, with its overgrown hedges and rusted metal lawn chairs, seemed dreary. When I came back inside, light and air bursting in with me, Grandma, her hair up in a gray bun, would rock a little and smile. I would lean then against my mother's chair, Grandma's fond eyes peering at me, and whisper out of the corner of my mouth, "Mom, can we go?"

16. From the overall context of the passage, it is most likely that the word *lamentable* at the beginning of the third paragraph, means
  a. laughable.
  b. sad.
  c. insane.
  d. inspired.

17. Which of the following does the radar screen image underscore?
  a. the narrator's absorption in gadgets and the modern world
  b. the narrator's daydreaming nature
  c. the narrator's uneasy sense of herself in the same lineage as her mother and grandmother
  d. all of the above

18. In revising this story, the author is considering taking out the reference to "butterscotch and bitter sticks" and instead describing the candy as "bitter with a sweet under-taste." Which is better—the original or this alternative description—and why?
  a. the original, because it leaves the actual taste up to the reader's imagination
  b. the original, because it is more vivid and exact
  c. the alternative, because it is more brief and to the point
  d. the alternative, because it is more vivid and exact

19. Assume this piece is fiction and could have been written from any point of view. What would a switch to third person achieve?
  a. Readers would be somewhat distanced from the narrator's feelings.
  b. The author would have more latitude to express the narrator's feelings.
  c. Readers would be more likely to identify with the feelings expressed.
  d. The grandmother's feelings would become more apparent.

20. In a previous version of this story, the author described the garden as having "lush hedges and quaint metal chairs." Why is it more effective to describe the hedges as "overgrown" and the chairs as "rusted"?
  a. These words add to the sense of age lingering over the place.
  b. These words have a negative connotation, which mirrors the girl's feelings about the visits.
  c. These words make the garden seem like less of an escape than the girl had hoped for.
  d. all of the above

21. Which of the following accurately reflects the comparative attitudes of the characters in this excerpt?
  a. The attitudes of the mother and the daughter are similar.
  b. The attitudes of the grandmother and the mother are similar.
  c. The attitudes of the grandmother and the granddaughter are similar.
  d. The attitudes of the mother and the daughter are dissimilar.

"The Wolf and the Crane"

A wolf who had a bone stuck in his throat hired a crane, for a large sum, to put her head into his mouth and draw out the bone. When the crane had extracted the bone and demanded the promised payment, the wolf, grinning and grinding his teeth, exclaimed: "Why you have surely already had a sufficient recompense, in having been permitted to draw out your head in safety from the mouth and jaws of a wolf."

22. Following is a list of morals from this and other Aesop fables. Which one is the most likely companion to this fable?
  a. Self-help is the best help.
  b. The loiterer often blames delay on his more active friend.
  c. The greatest kindness will not bind the ungrateful.
  d. In serving the wicked, expect no reward.

Fly-Rights—A Consumer Guide to Air Travel
(excerpt)

If your reservations are booked far enough ahead of time, the airline may offer to mail your tickets to you. However, if you don't receive the tickets and the airline's records show that they mailed them, you may have to go through cumbersome lost-ticket procedures. It is safer to check the telephone directory for a conveniently located travel agency or airline ticket office and buy your tickets there.

As soon as you receive your ticket, make sure all the information on it is correct, especially the airports (if any of the cities have more than one) and the flight dates. Have any necessary corrections made immediately.

It's a good idea to reconfirm your reservations before you start your trip; flight schedules sometimes change. On international trips, most airlines require that you reconfirm your onward or return reservations at least 72 hours before each flight. If you don't, your reservations may be canceled.

Check your tickets as you board each flight to ensure that only the correct coupon has been removed by the airline agent.

23. Numbering the paragraphs 1 through 4 as they now appear, choose the option that places them in chronological order.
  a. 2, 3, 4, 1
  b. 3, 1, 2, 4
  c. 3, 2, 1, 4
  d. 1, 2, 3, 4

24. Notice that this manual is written in the second person, employing the "you" pronoun. Considering the purpose of the manual, is this the best choice and why?
  a. Yes, because it avoids the necessity to choose between male and female pronouns.
  b. Yes, because the people who will be doing the traveling are addressed directly.
  c. No, because not all people travel by plane.
  d. No, because it makes readers unnecessarily uncomfortable to be addressed directly.

25. As the passage appears in paragraph 1, why is it suggested that you buy your tickets from a "conveniently located" agency or office?
  a. because you can stop on your way to the airport to pick up your tickets
  b. because you can pick your tickets up rather than relying on the mail
  c. because the airlines themselves often make mistakes in issuing tickets
  d. because it is good to support local businesses

26. Which is a possible result of not following the advice offered in the first sentence of paragraph 2?
  a. You might fly into the right city, but the wrong airport.
  b. You might miss your flight, because the date was improperly recorded.
  c. You might not be allowed to board your flight because the name on the ticket doesn't match that on your ID.
  d. Any of the above could happen as a result of not following the advice.

"Bear Story"

Campers Gene and Marie Marsden took pride in being good citizens when in the wild. While driving the three hundred miles from their home in Colorado to the Green River Lakes area of the Wind River Mountains in Wyoming, they instructed their children in the protocol they'd learned in the bear safety pamphlet put out by the Bridger-Teton Forest Service. The number-one rule was "Don't feed the bears!"—whether intentionally or not. Warning the kids not to go anywhere near a bear, the Marsdens had no problem with the intentional part, but the unintentional part was not as easy to avoid as they thought.

Mr. and Mrs. Marsden did their best to keep a tidy camp. While the bear manual had said to hang all food at least ten feet off the ground and four feet out from the trunk of a tree, they did what all the other people in the nearby public campground were doing and locked their food in their little utility trailer at night. Afraid that the scent of the bait might attract a bear, they even locked up Marie's fishing pole. It was always dark when they went to bed, but they perused the campsite with flashlights, making sure nothing was left out. Taking the recommended precaution of sleeping a hundred yards from where they cooked their food, they kept the car near their tents, unhitched from the trailer, which they left up at the other camp. Before going to bed each night, all of the Marsdens took off the clothes they had worn during the day while eating, replacing them with pajamas that they used only for sleeping. They were also careful to lock the dirty laundry in the trailer. As the pamphlet advised, they took no snacks into their tents.

Gene says he now regrets not having taken their dog into the tent at night, but they liked having him on guard. Small animals would often come sniffing around, and the dog would chase them back into the thickets, then return to the hollow he'd dug for himself in front of the children's tent. But on the night of the encounter, Spike would not stop barking, and Marie Marsden knew he must be sounding the alarm on something more dangerous and dauntless than a raccoon or squirrel. When she unzipped the tent and shined her flashlight in the direction of the cooking area, she saw Spike attempting to hold a young grizzly bear at bay.

They all managed to pile into the car, and with the kids sitting atop stuffed sacks full of clothes and gear, they drove quickly down the trail, calling out the window to Spike and abandoning the cargo trailer to whatever fate the bear might have in store for it. Uncertain whether the bear was following, one of the children opened a door and loaded Spike up on the run. They drove to a pay phone twenty miles away and called a Fish and Game Department ranger, who identified the bear by the white ruff the Marsdens had seen around his neck. The authorities informed the Marsdens that the bear was a young, recently weaned male that they'd been keeping an eye on.

The next morning, the Marsdens heard helicopters circling over the mountain above them and wondered if it might have something to do with the bear. After spending the night in the public campground, they drove back to their site. Wandering the area in search of clues, Marie came to a halt below the tallest spruce. She slapped her head and shouted, "Oh no!"

"What is it?" Gene asked.

Marie pointed at the ground where Spike's dog food bowl lay upside down.

A week after their return home, the Marsdens read the headline in their local paper. "Bear Euthanized in Wind Rivers." According to the article, the Fish and Game Department had shot the young bear because, having been rewarded for invading a human campsite, it would likely do so again.

The Marsdens knew they had been lucky in the encounter, yet much to their shame and sadness, they also knew that the bear had not.

27. Which of the following statements is true?
  a. The Marsdens went camping in the Wind River Mountains of Wyoming.
  b. The pamphlet on camping in bear country was sent to the Marsdens by the Fish and Game Department.
  c. The Marsdens went camping in the Green River Lakes area near their hometown.
  d. all of the above

28. Who does the author imply is mostly to blame in the bear's death?
  a. the Marsdens, because they were not careful enough
  b. the bear, because he invaded a human camp
  c. the Fish and Game authorities, because of poor communication with campers
  d. the Forest Service, for putting out incomplete information

29. In paragraph 2, it can be determined from the context that the word "perused" means
  a. neglected.
  b. cleaned.
  c. studied.
  d. hid.

30. In paragraph 3, it can be determined from the context that the word "dauntless" means
  a. stupid.
  b. fearless.
  c. clumsy.
  d. spineless.

31. This story is arranged
  a. like a news story, with the most important event told first.
  b. in reverse chronological order, with the last event first.
  c. in standard chronological order, with events told in the order they occurred.
  d. in mixed, random order.

32. What was the "reward" referred to in the next to last paragraph?
  a. the bear seeing the Marsdens run from him
  b. the bear receiving no punishment for disturbing humans
  c. the bear being able to stand off Spike
  d. the bear getting the dog food

33. The tone and style of this piece make it appropriate for which of the following types of publications?
  a. a scientific report on human-bear interaction
  b. a pamphlet on bear safety such as the one the Marsdens read
  c. a statistical study on bear fatalities in the Western mountains
  d. a human interest article in the Sunday magazine of a newspaper

"A Plains Childhood"

When I think of my family's history on the land, I experience a pang of regret. Unlike much of the arid West, where the land has gone virtually unchanged for centuries, my place of origin, western Kansas, has been torn up by agriculture. The flat plains, excellent soil, and sparse but just adequate rainfall permitted farming; therefore farming prevailed, and a good 90% of the original sod prairie is gone. The consequence, in human terms, is that our relationship to our place has always felt primarily mercantile. We used the land and denied, or held at bay, its effect on us. Yet from my earliest childhood, when most of the Kansas prairie was still intact, I've known that the land also had a romantic quality. I've felt moved by the expanse of it, enthralled by its size. I take pride in my identity as a plains daughter.

34. Which of the following is the most accurate restatement of the author's position?
  a. The presence of people has enriched the plains habitat.
  b. Farming has improved the soil of the plains.
  c. Farming has eroded the natural beauty of the plains.
  d. Farming has chemically polluted the plains.

35. The argument in this paragraph is based primarily on
  a. facts of history and statistical studies.
  b. facts derived from the author's personal observations.
  c. feelings the author has picked up from personal experience.
  d. feelings passed down to the author by ancestors.

36. From context, it can be determined that the word "mercantile" has something to do with
  a. practicality.
  b. danger.
  c. America.
  d. spirituality.

The coast of the State of Maine is one of the most irregular in the world. A straight line running from the southernmost coastal city to the northernmost coastal city would measure about 225 miles. If you followed the coastline between these points, you would travel more than ten times as far. This irregularity is the result of what is called a drowned coastline. The term comes from the glacial activity of the Ice Age. At that time, the whole area that is now Maine was part of a mountain range that towered above the sea. As the glacier descended, however, it expended enormous force on those mountains, and they sank into the sea.

As the mountains sank, ocean water charged over the lowest parts of the remaining land, forming a series of twisting inlets and lagoons of contorted grottos and nooks. The highest parts of the former mountain range, nearest the shore, remained as islands. Mt. Desert Island was one of the most famous of all the islands left behind by the glacier. Marine fossils found here were 225 feet above sea level indicating the level of the shoreline prior to the glacier.

The 2,500 mile long rocky and jagged coastline of Maine keeps watch over nearly 2,000 islands. Many of these islands are tiny and uninhabited, but many are home to thriving communities. Mt. Desert Island is one of the largest, most beautiful of the Maine coast islands. Measuring 16 miles by 12 miles, Mt. Desert was very nearly formed as two distinct islands. It is split almost in half by Somes Sound, a very deep and very narrow stretch of water seven miles long.

For years, Mt. Desert Island, particularly its major settlement, Bar Harbor, afforded summer homes for the wealthy. Recently though, Bar Harbor has become a burgeoning arts community as well. But, the best part of the island is the unspoiled forest land known as Acadia National Park. Since the island sits on the boundary line between the temperate and subarctic zones, the island supports the <u>flora and fauna</u> of both zones as well as beach, inland, and alpine plants. It also lies in a major bird migration lane and is a resting spot for many birds.

The establishment of Acadia National Park in 1916 means that this natural monument will be preserved and that it will be available to all people, not just the wealthy. Visitors to Acadia may receive nature instruction from the park naturalists as well as enjoy camping, hiking, cycling, and boating. Or they may choose to spend time at the archeological museum learning about the Stone Age inhabitants of the island.

The best view on Mt. Desert Island is from the top of Cadillac Mountain. This mountain rises 1,532 feet, making it the highest mountain on the Atlantic seaboard. From the summit, you can gaze back toward the mainland or out over the Atlantic Ocean and contemplate the beauty created by a retreating glacier.

37. Which of the following lists of topics best outlines the information in the selection?
  a. — Ice-Age glacial activity
     — The Islands of Casco Bay
     — Formation of Cadillac Mountain
     — Summer residents of Mt. Desert Island
  b. — Formation of a drowned coastline
     — The topography of Mt. Desert Island
     — The environment of Mt. Desert Island
     — Tourist attractions on Mt. Desert Island
  c. — Mapping the Maine coastline
     — The arts community at Bar Harbor
     — History of the National Park system
     — Climbing Cadillac Mountain
  d. — The effect of glaciers on small islands
     — Stone-Age dwellers on Mt. Desert Island
     — The importance of biodiversity
     — Hiking in Acadia National Park

38. Which of the following statements best expresses the main idea of paragraph 4 of the selection?
  a. The wealthy residents of Mt. Desert Island selfishly kept it to themselves.
  b. Acadia National Park is one of the smallest of the national parks.
  c. On Mt. Desert Island, there is great tension between the year-round residents and the summer tourists.
  d. Due to its location and environment, Mt. Desert Island supports an incredibly diverse animal and plant life.

39. According to the selection, the large number of small islands along the coast of Maine are the result of
  a. glaciers forcing a mountain range into the sea.
  b. Maine's location between the temperate and subarctic zones.
  c. the irregularity of the Maine coast.
  d. the need for summer communities for wealthy tourists and artists.

40. The content of paragraph 5 indicates that the writer believes that
  a. the continued existence of national parks is threatened by budget cuts.
  b. the best way to preserve the environment on Mt. Desert Island is to limit the number of visitors.
  c. national parks allow large numbers of people to visit and learn about interesting wilderness areas.
  d. Mt. Desert Island is the most interesting tourist attraction in Maine.

41. According to the selection, the coast of Maine is
  a. 2,500 miles long.
  b. 3,500 miles long.
  c. 225 miles long.
  d. 235 miles long.

42. What is the meaning of the underlined phrase flora and fauna in paragraph 4 of this passage?
  a. insects and plants
  b. plants and animals
  c. deer and coyote
  d. birds and beaches

The immune system is equal in complexity to the combined <u>intricacies</u> of the brain and nervous system. The success of the immune system in defending the body relies on a dynamic regulatory communications network consisting of millions and millions of cells. Organized into sets and subsets, these cells pass information back and forth like clouds of bees swarming around a hive. The result is a sensitive system of checks and balances that produces an immune response that is prompt, appropriate, effective, and self-limiting.

At the heart of the immune system is the ability to distinguish between self and nonself. When immune defenders encounter cells or organisms carrying foreign or nonself molecules, the immune troops move quickly to eliminate the intruders. Virtually every body cell carries distinctive molecules that identify it as self. The body's immune defenses do not normally attack tissues that carry a self-marker. Rather, immune cells and other body cells coexist peaceably in a state known as self-tolerance. When a normally functioning immune system attacks a nonself molecule, the system has the ability to "remember" the specifics of the foreign body. Upon subsequent encounters with the same species of molecules, the immune system reacts accordingly. With the possible exception of antibodies passed during lactation, this so called immune system memory is not inherited. Despite the occurrence of a virus in your family, your immune system must "learn" from experience with the many millions of distinctive nonself molecules in the sea of microbes in which we live. Learning entails producing the appropriate molecules and cells to match up with and counteract each nonself invader.

Any substance capable of triggering an immune response is called an antigen. Antigens are not to be confused with allergens, which are most often harmless substances (such as ragweed pollen or cat hair) that provoke the immune system to set off the inappropriate and harmful response known as allergy. An antigen can be a virus, a bacterium, a fungus, a parasite, or even a portion or product of one of these organisms. Tissues or cells from another individual (except an identical twin, whose cells carry identical self-markers) also act as antigens; because the immune system recognizes transplanted tissues as foreign, it rejects them. The body will even reject nourishing proteins unless they are first broken down by the digestive system into their primary, nonantigenic building blocks. An antigen announces its foreignness by means of intricate and characteristic shapes called epitopes, which protrude from its surface. Most antigens, even the simplest microbes, carry several different kinds of epitopes on their surface; some may even carry several hundred. Some epitopes will be more effective than others at stimulating an immune response. Only in abnormal situations does the immune system wrongly identify self as nonself and execute a misdirected immune attack. The result can be a so-called autoimmune disease such as rheumatoid arthritis or systemic lupus erythematosis. The painful side effects of these diseases are caused by a person's immune system actually attacking itself.

43. What is the analogy used to describe the communications network among the cells in the immune system?
   a. the immune system's memory
   b. immune troops eliminating intruders
   c. bees swarming around a hive
   d. a sea of microbes

44. The immune cells and other cells in the body coexist peaceably in a state known as
   a. equilibrium.
   b. self-tolerance.
   c. harmony.
   d. tolerance.

45. What is the specific term for the substance capable of triggering an inappropriate or harmful immune response to a harmless substance such as ragweed pollen?
   a. antigen
   b. microbe
   c. allergen
   d. autoimmune disease

46. How do the cells in the immune system recognize an antigen as "foreign" or "nonself?"
   a. through an allergic response
   b. through blood type
   c. through fine hairs protruding from the antigen surface
   d. through characteristic shapes on the antigen surface

47. After you have had the chicken pox, your immune system will be able to do all of the following EXCEPT
   a. prevent your offspring from infection by the chicken pox virus.
   b. distinguish between your body cells and that of the chicken pox virus.
   c. "remember" previous experiences with the chicken pox virus.
   d. match up and counteract nonself molecules in the form of the chicken pox virus.

48. Which of the following best expresses the main idea of this passage?
   a. An antigen is any substance that triggers an immune response.
   b. The basic function of the immune system is to distinguish between self and nonself.
   c. One of the immune system's primary functions is the allergic response.
   d. The human body presents an opportune habitat for microbes.

49. Why would tissue transplanted from father to daughter have a greater risk of being detected as foreign than a tissue transplanted between identical twins?
   a. The age of the twins' tissue would be the same and therefore less likely to be rejected.
   b. The identical twin's tissue would carry the same self-markers and would therefore be less likely to be rejected.
   c. The difference in the sex of the father and daughter would cause the tissue to be rejected by the daughter's immune system.
   d. The twins' immune systems would "remember" the same encounters with childhood illnesses.

50. What is the meaning of the underlined word intricacies as it is used in the first sentence of the passage?
   a. elaborate interconnections
   b. confusion of pathways
   c. inherent perplexity
   d. comprehensive coverage

▶ Answer Key

1. c. Lesson 3	**26.** d. Lesson 17
2. b. Lesson 1	**27.** a. Lesson 1
3. b. Lesson 18	**28.** a. Lesson 16
4. c. Lesson 2	**29.** c. Lesson 3
5. a. Lesson 8	**30.** b. Lesson 3
6. c. Lesson 14	**31.** c. Lesson 6
7. d. Lesson 1	**32.** d. Lesson 16
8. a. Lesson 1	**33.** d. Lesson 13
9. b. Lesson 2	**34.** c. Lesson 16
10. c. Lesson 8	**35.** c. Lesson 4
11. c. Lesson 4	**36.** a. Lesson 3
12. d. Lesson 12	**37.** b. Lesson 1
13. c. Lesson 3	**38.** d. Lesson 2
14. d. Lesson 11	**39.** a. Lesson 9
15. a. Lesson 4	**40.** c. Lesson 4
16. b. Lesson 3	**41.** a. Lesson 1
17. c. Lesson 12	**42.** b. Lesson 3
18. b. Lesson 13	**43.** c. Lesson 8
19. a. Lesson 11	**44.** b. Lesson 1
20. d. Lesson 12	**45.** c. Lesson 3
21. a. Lesson 8	**46.** d. Lesson 9
22. d. Lesson 16	**47.** a. Lesson 6
23. d. Lesson 6	**48.** b. Lesson 2
24. b. Lesson 11	**49.** b. Lesson 9
25. b. Lesson 16	**50.** a. Lesson 3

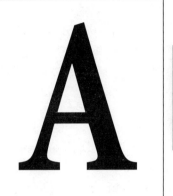

Preparing for a Standardized Test

Most of us get nevous about tests, especially standardized tests, where our scores can have a significant impact on our future. Nervousness is natural—and it can even be an advantage if you know how to channel it into positive energy.

The following pages provide suggestions for overcoming test anxiety both in the days and weeks before the test and during the test itself.

▶ Two to Three Months before the Test

The number one best way to combat test anxiety is to **be prepared.** That means two things: Know what to expect on the test and review the material and skills on which you will be tested.

Know What to Expect
What knowledge or skills will the exam test? What are you expected to know? What skills will you be expected to demonstrate? What is the format of the test? Multiple choice? True or false? Essay? If possible, go to a bookstore

or the library for a study guide that shows you what a sample test looks like. Or maybe the agency that's testing you for a job offers a study guide or conducts study sessions. The fewer surprises you have on test day, the better you will perform. And the more you know what to expect, the more confident you will be to handle the questions.

Review the Material and Skills You'll Be Tested On

The fact that you are reading this book means that you've already taken this step. Now, are there other steps you can take? Are there other subject areas you need to review? Can you make more improvement in this or other areas? If you are really nervous or if it has been a long time since you reviewed these subjects and skills, you may want to buy another study guide, sign up for a class in your neighborhood, or work with a tutor.

The more you know about what to expect on test day and the more comfortable you are with the material and skills to be tested, the less anxious you will be and the better you will do on the test itself.

▶ The Days before the Test

Review, Don't Cram

If you have been preparing and reviewing in the weeks before the exam, there's no need to cram a few days beforehand. Cramming is likely to confuse you and make you nervous. Instead, schedule a relaxed review of all you have learned.

Physical Activity

Get some exercise in the days preceding the test. You'll send some extra oxygen to your brain and allow your thinking performance to peak on the day you take the test. Moderation is the key here. Don't exercise so much that you feel exhausted, but a little physical activity will invigorate your body and brain. Walking is a terrific, low-impact, energy-building form of exercise.

Balanced Diet

Like your body, your brain needs proper nutrients to function well. Eat plenty of fruits and vegetables in the days before the test. Foods high in lecithin, such as fish and beans, are especially good choices. Lecithin is a protein your brain needs for peak performance. You may even consider a visit to your local pharmacy to buy a bottle of lecithin tablets several weeks before your test.

Rest

Get plenty of sleep the nights before the test. Don't overdo it, though, or you'll make yourself as groggy as if you were overtired. Go to bed at a reasonable time, early enough to get the hours of rest you need to function **effectively**. You'll feel relaxed and rested if you've gotten plenty of sleep in the days before you take the test.

Trial Run

At some point before the test, make a trial run to the testing center to see how long it takes to get there. Rushing raises your emotional energy and lowers your intellectual capacity, so you want to allow plenty of time on test day to get to the testing center. Arriving ten or fifteen minutes early gives you time to relax and get situated.

Motivation

Plan some sort of celebration—with family or friends, or just by yourself—for after the test. Make sure it's something you'll really look forward to and enjoy. If you have something planned for after the test, you may find it easier to prepare and keep moving during the test.

▶ Test Day

It's finally here, the day of the big test. Set your alarm early enough to allow plenty of time to get to the testing center. Eat a good breakfast. Avoid anything that's really high in sugar, such as donuts. A sugar high turns into a sugar low after an hour or so. Cereal and toast, or anything with complex carbohydrates is a good choice. Eat only moderate amounts. You don't want to take a test feeling stuffed! Your body will channel its energy to your digestive system instead of your brain.

Pack a high-energy snack to take with you. You may have a break sometime during the test when you can grab a quick snack. Bananas are great. They have a moderate amount of sugar and plenty of brain nutrients, such as potassium. Most proctors won't allow you to eat a snack while you're testing, but a peppermint shouldn't pose a problem. Peppermints are like smelling salts for your brain. If you lose your concentration or suffer from a momentary mental block, a peppermint can get you back on track. Don't forget the earlier advice about relaxing and taking a few deep breaths.

Leave early enough so you have plenty of time to get to the test center. Allow a few minutes for unexpected traffic. When you arrive, locate the restroom and use it. Few things interfere with concentration as much as a full bladder. Then find your seat and make sure it's comfortable. If it isn't, tell the proctor and ask to move to something more suitable.

Now relax and think positively! Before you know it, the test will be over, and you'll walk away knowing you've done as well as you can.

▶ Combating Test Anxiety

Okay—you know what the test will be on. You've reviewed the subjects and practiced the skills on which you will be tested. So why do you still have that sinking feeling in your stomach? Why are your palms sweaty and your hands shaking?

Even the brightest, most well-prepared test takers sometimes suffer bouts of test anxiety. But don't worry; you can overcome it. Here are some specific strategies to help you.

Take the Test One Question at a Time

Focus all your attention on the one question you're answering. Avoid thoughts about questions you've already read or concerns about what's coming next. Concentrate your thinking where it will do the most good—on the question you're answering now.

Develop a Positive Attitude

Keep reminding yourself that you're prepared. In fact, if you've read this book or any other in the LearningExpress Skill Builders series, you're probably better prepared than most other test takers. Remember, it's only a test, and you will do your **best**. That's all anyone can ask of you. If that nagging drill sergeant voice inside your head starts sending negative messages, combat them with positive ones of your own. Tell yourself:

- "I'm doing just fine."
- "I've prepared for this test."
- "I know exactly what to do."
- "I know I can get the score I'm shooting for."

You get the idea. Remember to drown out negative messages with positive ones of your own.

If You Lose Your Concentration

Don't worry about it! It's normal. During a long test, it happens to everyone. When your mind is stressed or overexerted, it takes a break whether you want it to or not. It's easy to get your concentration back if you simply acknowledge the fact that you've lost it and take a quick break. You brain needs very little time (seconds, really) to rest.

Put your pencil down and close your eyes. Take a deep breath, hold it for a moment, and let it out slowly. Listen to the sound of your breathing as you repeat this two more times. The few seconds this takes is really all the time your brain needs to relax and refocus. This exercise also helps you control your heart rate, so you can keep anxiety at bay.

Try this technique several times before the test when you feel stressed. The more you practice, the better it will work for you on test day.

If You Freeze

Don't worry about a question that stumps you even though you're sure you know the answer. Mark it and go on to the next question. You can come back to the "stumper" later. Try to put it out of your mind completely until you come back to it. Just let your subconscious mind chew on the question while your conscious mind focuses on the other items (one at a time—of course). Chances are, the memory block will be gone by the time you return to the question.

If you freeze before you ever begin the test, here's what to do:

1. Do some deep breathing to help yourself relax and focus.
2. Remind yourself that you're prepared.
3. Take some time to look over the test.
4. Read a few of the questions.
5. Decide which ones are the easiest and start there.

Before long, you'll be "in the groove."

▶ Time Strategies

One of the most important—and nerve-wracking—elements of a standardized test is time. You'll only be allowed a certain number of minutes for each section, so it is very important that you use your time wisely.

Pace Yourself

The most important time strategy is **pacing yourself**. Before you begin, take just a few seconds to survey the test, noting the number of questions and the sections that look easier than the rest. Then, make a rough time schedule based on the amount of time available to you. Mark the halfway point on your test and make a note beside that mark of the time when the testing period is half over.

Keep Moving

Once you begin the test, **keep moving**. If you work slowly in an attempt to make fewer mistakes, your mind will become bored and begin to wander. You'll end up making far more mistakes if you're not concentrating. Worse, if you take too long to answer questions that stump you, you may end up running out of time before you finish.

So don't stop for difficult questions. Skip them and move on. You can come back to them later if you have time. A question that takes you five seconds to answer counts as much as one that takes you several minutes, so pick up the easy points first. Besides, answering the easier questions first helps build your confidence and gets you in the testing groove. Who knows? As you go through the test, you may even stumble across some relevant information to help you answer those tough questions.

Don't Rush

Keep moving, but **don't rush**. Think of your mind as a seesaw. On one side is your emotional energy; on the other side, your intellectual energy. When your emotional energy is high, your intellectual capacity is low. Remember how difficult it is to reason with someone when you're angry? On the other hand, when your intellectual energy is high, your emotional energy is low. Rushing raises your emotional energy and reduces your intellectual capacity. Remember the last time you were late for work? All that rushing around probably caused you to forget important things—like your lunch. Move quickly to keep your mind from wandering, but don't rush and get yourself flustered.

Check Yourself

Check yourself at the halfway mark. If you're a little ahead, you know you're on track and may even have a little time left to check your work. If you're a little behind, you have several choices. You can pick up the pace a little, but do this *only* if you can do it comfortably. Remember—**don't rush!** You can also skip around in the remaining portion of the test to pick up as many easy points as possible. This strategy has one drawback, however. If you are marking a bubble-style answer sheet, and you put the right answers in the wrong bubbles—they're wrong. So pay close attention to the question numbers if you decide to do this.

▶ Avoiding Errors

When you take the test, you want to make as few errors as possible in the questions you answer. Here are a few tactics to keep in mind.

Control Yourself

Remember that comparison between your mind and a seesaw? Keeping your emotional energy low and your intellectual energy high is the best way to avoid mistakes. If you feel stressed or worried, stop for a few seconds. Acknowledge the feeling (Hmmm! I'm feeling a little pressure here!), take a few deep breaths, and send yourself a few positive messages. This relieves your emotional anxiety and boosts your intellectual capacity.

Directions

In many standardized testing situations, a proctor reads the instructions aloud. Make certain you understand what is expected. If you don't, **ask**. Listen carefully for instructions about how to answer the questions and make certain you know how much time you have to complete the task. Write the time on your test if you don't already know how long you have to take the test. If you miss this vital information, **ask for it**. You need it to do well on your test.

Answers

This may seem like a silly warning, but it is important. Place your answers in the right blanks or the corresponding ovals on the answer sheet. Right answers in the wrong place earn no points—you may even lose points. It's a good idea to check every five to ten questions to make sure you're in the right spot. That way, you won't need much time to correct your answer sheet if you have made an error.

Choosing the Right Answers by Process of Elimination

Make sure you understand what the question is asking. If you're not sure of what's being asked, you'll never know whether you've chosen the right answer. So determine what the question is asking. If the answer isn't readily apparent, look for clues in the answer choices. Notice the similarities and differences in the answer choices. Sometimes, this helps to put the question in a new perspective, making it easier to answer. If you're still not sure of the answer, use the process of elimination. First, eliminate any answer choices that obviously wrong. Then, reason your way through the remaining choices. You may be able to use relevant information from other parts of the test. If you can't eliminate any of the answer choices, you might be better off to skip the question and come back to it later. If you can't eliminate any answer choices to improve your odds when you return, make a guess and move on.

If You're Penalized for Wrong Answers

You **must know** whether there's a penalty for wrong answers before you begin the test. If you don't, ask the proctor before the test begins. Whether you make a guess depends on the penalty. Some standardized tests are scored in such a way that every wrong answer reduces your score by one-fourth or one-half of a point. Whatever the penalty, if you can eliminate enough choices to make the odds of answering the question better than the penalty for getting it wrong, make a guess.

Let's imagine you are taking a test in which each answer has four choices and you are penalized one-fourth of a point for each wrong answer. If you have no clue and cannot eliminate any of the answer choices, you're better off leaving the question blank because the odds of answering correctly are one in four. This makes the penalty and the odds equal. However, if you can eliminate one of the choices, the odds are now in your favor. You have a one in three chance of answering the question correctly. Fortunately, few tests are scored using such elaborate means, but if your test is one of them, know the penalties and calculate your odds before you take a guess on a question.

If You Finish Early

Use any time you have left at the end of the test or test section to check your work. First, make certain you've put the answers in the right places. As you're doing this, make sure you've answered each question only once. Most standardized tests are scored in such a way that questions with more than one answer are marked wrong. If you've erased an answer, make sure you've done a good job. Check for stray marks on your answer sheet that could distort your score.

After you've checked for these obvious errors, take a second look at the more difficult questions. You've probably heard the folk wisdom about never changing an answer. It's not always good advice. If you have a good reason for thinking a response is wrong, change it.

► After the Test

Once you've finished, *congratulate yourself.* You've worked hard to prepare; now it's time to enjoy yourself and relax. Remember that celebration you planned before the test? Go to it!

B ▶ Additional Resources

Reading is like exercise: If you don't keep doing it, you'll get out of shape. Like muscles that grow stronger and bigger with each repetition, your reading skills grow stronger and stronger with everything you read. But if you stop working out, your reading comprehension muscles will deteriorate, and you may find yourself struggling with material you could have easily understood several months ago.

So don't stop now! You've really just begun. Reading comprehension is a skill to build throughout your whole lifetime.

▶ Tips for Continuing to Improve Your Reading

The following are some ways you can continue to strengthen your reading comprehension skills:

- **Read!** Read anything—books, newspapers, magazines, novels, poems. The more you read, the better. Set yourself a reading goal: one book a month, two books while you're on vacation, a half hour of reading every night before bed. There's a list of suggested books at the end of this section; try some.

- **Discover new authors.** Check out the best-seller list and try the books on that list. If it's a best-seller, it's probably a book that appeals to a wide variety of readers, and chances are, you'll like it.
- **Spend time in bookstores and libraries.** There are bound to be books and authors out there that appeal to some of your interests. Don't be afraid to ask a salesperson or librarian to help you: Describe your interests and your preferences in style, and he or she can help you find books you'll enjoy reading.
- **Join a reading group.** Most cities and towns have a club that meets every two weeks or each month to discuss a selected book. In these groups, you'll be able to discuss your ideas and questions with a group of friends and associates in an informal setting. If your area doesn't have a reading group, start your own. You and your friends can take turns choosing which book you'll read and discuss.
- **Review this book periodically to refresh yourself about the basics.** Try some of the skill building exercises at the end of each lesson on a regular basis.

▶ Suggested Reading List

On the following pages is a list of great reads. These suggestions is just the tip of the iceberg! It is broken down into different subjects, so try reading some of the books in the categories that interest you.

Autobiography

A Moveable Feast by Ernest Hemingway
I Know Why the Caged Bird Sings by Maya Angelou
My Life by Bill Clinton
Narrative of the Life of Frederick Douglass, an American Slave by Frederick Douglass
Night by Elie Wiesel
The Story of My Life by Helen Keller

Coming of Age

Catcher in the Rye by J.D. Salinger
Great Expectations by Charles Dickens
Little Women by Louisa May Alcott
Peace Like a River by Leif Engler

Historical/Social Issues

One Flew Over the Cuckoo's Nest by Ken Kesey
Pride and Prejudice by Jane Austen
Raisin in the Sun by Lorraine Hansberry
The Bluest Eye by Toni Morrison
The Grapes of Wrath by John Steinbeck

Inspirational/Spiritual

Awake My Soul: Spirituality for Busy People by Timothy K. Jones
Da Vinci Code by Dan Brown
Simple Path by Mother Theresa
The Five People You Meet in Heaven by Mitch Albom
The Prayer of Jabez: Breaking Through to the Blessed Life by Bruce Wilkinson
The Purpose-Drive Life: What on Earth Am I Here For? by Rick Warren

Mystery/Thriller

2nd Chance by James Patterson
American Psycho by Bret Easton Ellis
On the Street Where You Live by Mary Higgins Clark
State of Fear by Michael Crichton
The Godfather by Mario Puzo

Poetry

Collected Poems of Langston Hughes by Langston Hughes
The Collected Poems of Emily Dickinson by Emily Dickinson
The Sonnets by William Shakespeare
The Vintage Book of Contemporary American Poetry by J.D. McClatchy
Walt Whitman: Poetry and Prose by Walt Whitman

Science Fiction/Fantasy

Brave New World by Aldous Huxley

Frankenstein by Mary Shelley

Harry Potter (series) by J.K. Rowling

Lord of the Rings (trilogy) by J.R.R. Tolkien

Strange Case of Dr. Jekyll and Mr. Hyde by Robert Louis Stevenson

Short Stories

Demonology: Stories by Rick Moody

Drinking Coffee Elsewhere by Z.Z. Packer

Everything's Eventual: 14 Dark Tales by Stephen King

The Complete Tales and Poems of Edgar Allan Poe by Edgar Allan Poe

Science/Health

Bioterrorism and Public Health by John G. Bartlett

Black Death: AIDS in Africa by Susan Hunter

Blood Evidence by Henry C. Lee

Cognitive Neuroscience: The Biology of the Mind by Michael S. Gazzaniga

War

Al-Qaeda: Casting a Shadow of Terror by Jason Burke

Black Hawk Down: A Story of Modern War by Mark Bowden

Born on the Fourth of July by Ron Kovic

FREE Online Practice from LearningExpress!

Let LearningExpress help you acquire essential reading comprehension skills FAST!

Go to the LearningExpress Practice Center at www.LearningExpressFreeOffer.com, an interactive online resource exclusively for LearningExpress customers.

Now that you've purchased LearningExpress's *Reading Comprehension Success in 20 Minutes a Day* skill-builder book, you have **FREE** access to:

- **50 exercises covering ALL VITAL READING COMPREHENSION SKILLS** that will test your understanding of passages, as well as how well you read
- **Immediate scoring** and **detailed answer explanations**
- Benchmark your skills and focus your study with our **customized diagnostic report**

Follow the simple instructions on the scratch card in your copy of *Reading Comprehension Success.* Use your individualzed access code found on the scratch card and go to www.LearningExpressFree Offer.com to log in. Start practicing your reading comprehension skills online right away!

Once you've logged on, use the spaces below to write in your access code and newly created password for easy reference:

Access Code: _____   Password: _____